Words of praise for

MW00827561

Jacquelyn D. Murray's *Oh, No...Not the Diva!* is a must-read book for anyone experiencing inner war between mental health issues and the church. Jacki walks her readers down a suppressed journey where physical illness meets and unleashes repressed trauma on a collision course with the unspoken beliefs regarding mental illness and the church. She challenges each reader that through basic heartfelt prayer and therapy, you, too, can let it go and trust God!

DR. JACQUELINE Y. FORD
Ph.D. Clinical Psychology and Author, *When the System Fails: Challenges of Child Trauma on Adoptive Families' Social and Emotional System*, Tucson, AZ

Today, we see mental illness abound and the impact has been devastating. But there is hope. No judgments. No criticism. Just help and healing. In *Oh, No...Not the Diva!* Jacki is honest and vulnerable. She shares her intimate struggles and challenges with mental illness with the heart to see others healed and restored as they, too, seek help. Her selfless act embodies the heart of God for His people in wanting them healed, restored, and whole. In my mind, the fact that she invites us close to her heart to see where she has been solidifies her as a woman of God with a big heart, larger than life. And yes, STILL the Diva!

DELLA STEIN,
Attorney, Orange County, CA

Oh, No...Not the Diva! is a great book that not only shares the testimony and life of Jacki, but also shows the vulnerability we all go through in different times of our lives. You will find yourself feeling the pain, fear, anger, and even neglect of her life that may even reveal what you have done or are doing now in your life. Her openness to communicate issues we deal with in and out of church will help you find a path to freedom just as Jacki did. I guarantee you can find nuggets of hope and faith that will help you.

ELI A. LOPEZ
Retired Assemblies of God Senior Pastor, Tucson, AZ

Oh, No...Not the Diva! courageously shines the light on the stigma of mental illness in the church and the African American community. This stigma often results in people internalizing their struggle with mental illness, resulting in isolation, suffering, and other negative consequences.

I am amazed at how Jacquelyn's transparency resonates with me as an individual, a pastor, and a marriage and family therapist. Many find it easy to empathize with someone who has cancer, a biological illness. The themes throughout this book clearly demonstrate that we must find a way to educate our community, including the church, in order to tear down stigmas and realize that PTSD, depression, bipolar disorder, etc. are psychological illnesses that require treatment and our empathy. To accept that someone has a mental illness is not denying the Lord or His power to heal!

Oh, No...Not the Diva! takes an empowering swing at blame and shame that leads us one step closer to dismantling the stereotypes and stigmas of mental illness. Instead, let us educate our families, our pastors, and our leaders on the impact of mental illness and what they can do to support a person who suffers from mental illness.

ALICIA PARTEE
Family Therapist, Global Counseling Solutions AS, Oslo, Norway

The issue of mental illness is a topic that is often ignored and avoided in our churches and the Christian community. It is the unspoken demon that no one wants to discuss or acknowledge, and many suffer in silence or denial while not realizing that help is just within their reach.

In her book, *Oh, No...Not the Diva!* Jacquelyn D. Murray provides an honest and vivid view of her personal journey with mental illness and how she is working to overcome this disease. I pray that her openness and transparency will give many in the church, especially women, the permission to open up about their own battle with the disease and to seek the necessary professional help to get healed.

I also pray that this book will be a wake-up call to the church to acknowledge that this is a disease that should not be ignored.

I pray that the church realizes that believers struggling should not be shunned but provided with a safe place to get the support and comfort needed to overcome mental illness, as we do with any other disease. Thank you, Jacki, for your bravery and for having the courage to share your story.

ANDREA SIMMONDS-KWAKYE
Speaker, San Jose, CA

This stimulating book is a must-read for anyone who is currently experiencing or has already gone through a life-changing event. Jacki uses relevant and relatable stories that capture your attention, liberate you from the place that occupies and restrains you, and extends comfort and healing to elevate and inspire you to go to a higher place. Her real-life stories gently transport you through her experiences to a place of ultimate healing. *Oh, No...Not the Diva!* will unlock and reveal the potentially unleashed future purposes for the reader.

Are you ready for your life to shift into a better place? If so, then this book is for you.

DR. AMANDA GOODSON
Author, Speaker, and Pastor of Trinity Temple CME, Tucson, AZ

It was too much, too fast. It was too real. *I'll either deal with it or I won't deal with it*, I decided, *and I probably won't deal with it because I don't know how to deal with it.*

With these and other thoughts, Jacki faces and begins to engage the challenge of some of life's most difficult realities: dysfunctional family relationships, marital disappointments, disjointed workplace arrangements, and potentially fatal health issues. We are permitted a behind the scenes and beneath the surface look at the heart of her crisis as Jacki comes to realize that at the core of her pains and perspectives are maladies she has never been exposed to, nor knew even existed.

With candor and courage, Jacki realizes and wrestles with the often-maligned and misrepresented symptoms and struggles of depression and PTSD. Her journey of acceptance and treatment of these often-maddening maladies, in the face of denial and criticism is at times tragic, but ultimately triumphant.

In finding her way, Jacki offers to the reader her painstaking pilgrimage and breakthrough in dealing with issues of mental illness, along with her commitment to treatment at the hands of professional therapies. You will be engaged in Jacki's journey as well as encouraged in your own.

REV. DR. HORACE W. SHEPPARD, JR.
Senior Pastor, Bethesda Christian Fellowship Church of God,
Philadelphia, PA

Oh, No...Not The Diva! is a riveting story of a Christ-centered woman whose life reflects the pain of childhood from an alcoholic father and a distant mother to becoming a young married and alone woman. Jacki shows us her bravery in using a seemingly unconventional approach to help her heal from past traumas which were a result of her being diagnosed with depression and mental illness. This story is absolutely life-altering; it will encourage and empower you that there is truly a light at the end of a dark tunnel. I highly recommend all clergy, church leaders, and anyone who is dealing with or has dealt with mental illness to read this book. *Oh, No...Not The Diva!* will ignite you to seek out professional help and gain understanding and empathy on how best to help and approach those in the Christian church who may be suffering in silence. It's time for churches to face this head on—and Jacki is leading the charge.

LORINDA MARTINEZ
Author, Speaker, Internet Radio Host, and Founder and CEO
of *New Beginnings with Lorinda*, Stockton, CA

Oh, No...Not the Diva! is a remarkable account of the struggles faced by many African American families but never discussed. Jacquelyn D. Murray does a remarkable job walking through the discovery of depression and how the symptoms often catch many people and families off guard, not knowing what to really do with them. As you read the story of Jacki, you will most likely find yourself in the pages as she shares what it's like to be in a dysfunctional family.

Carefully sharing the various co-dependent roles that family members often assume in alcoholic families causes parents and children to reassess their life responses to normal and traumatic situations. In most cases people assume this is "just the way they are" while not realizing how much trauma has impacted them. While taking a real hard look at herself, she faces her own dysfunction as she begins her journey of healing.

In many minority communities, things such as being diagnosed with depression, anxiety, and PTSD carries such a negative stigma that getting help usually never happens. Jacki's personal journey brings great insight on how "strong black women" or divas must face their "weaknesses" and accept that if "Superman" has a kryptonite, so can the Diva! If it's not enough to just face the dysfunction; she exposes the necessary therapies of medication, counseling, and EMDR treatment used to bring her the necessary healing needed.

As this no-holds-barred story unfolds, Jacki discloses the personal and intimate details often dealt with in the marriage, ministry, and the mind. This leaves her completely vulnerable in her account so others may find healing from her strength and example. As a specialist in trauma and marriage therapy, many people believe that it can be managed by faith alone in the context of family relationships and friends. She clearly reveals the ups and downs faced by many as they seek to find support and or even stay connected to those you would think would be expected to support them. This book causes the reader to take a real look at relationships and the impact of their actions on others who need their support and struggle to find it.

ARTHUR W. TIGNEY, JR.
Licensed Professional Counselor, NCC, Tucson, AZ

Oh, No...
Not the Diva!

Dealing and revealing while living with mental illness

Jacquelyn D. Murray

Oh, No...Not the Diva!
Dealing and revealing while living with mental illness

by Jacquelyn D. Murray

Adam Colwell's WriteWorks Publishing
Adam Colwell's WriteWorks LLC, Tucson, AZ

Edited by Adam Colwell and Dave Ficere
Cover design by Barney Hilton Murray
Typesetting by Katherine Lloyd, The DESK

Print ISBN: 978-0-9989587-8-1
eBook ISBN: 978-0-9989587-9-8

Dedication

On April 3, 2017, just a few months into this project, Mommy died. It was unexpected, and I can still hear the hysteria in my sister's voice as she gave me the news. My life changed forever on that day.

Mommy never knew of my diagnosis. You know how it goes—I like to say I didn't want to worry her. But the truth is I'm not sure she would have understood. But as a mother, I'm sure she knew something was wrong. Somewhere along this journey I began to understand so much more, not only about what I went through, but also some of what my mother dealt with. Bottom line, we both did the best we could with what we had. So it is with much love, admiration, and pride that I dedicate *Oh, No...Not the Diva!* to my mother. I love and miss you so much, Mommy.

Author's Note

All names used in this book, except my own, have been changed to protect the privacy of each individual. In addition, the details of my therapy sessions are not intended to be exact retellings, though they closely relate the actual dialogue and processes used.

Acknowledgments

This has been a difficult journey. Being vulnerable and transparent with my mental illness in *Oh, No...Not the Diva!* was a scary process to take on. But as always, the Lord helped me through to completion. And as always, He sent people along the way to encourage me.

Barney – You gave me a greeting card that said, "Sometimes life just doesn't make any sense. Bad things happen to good people, and we all wonder why. But even in those moments, some things remain true. God loves you and has a plan for your life." God has you in my life as part of that plan. Thank you for being there for me when I couldn't see my own way. I appreciate and love you very much.

Adam – We've done it once again! Thank you for believing in me and my story. Your support, guidance, and friendship have been a God-send.

Andrea – Thank you for your prayers and initial investment to help support this project and get me started. You've always been there for me and I am ever grateful for you and your friendship.

Sandra – My prayer partner, I know you're always going to pray! Thank you for keeping me before the Lord. Listening to my woes and often hearing my sobs has helped me to be able to get it out and move on. You'll never know how valuable your listening ear and kind heart are to me. I love you, Sis.

Amea – Buddy, you're the best! You've listened to a lot of my struggles along the way. Not once have you judged or put me down. You've always encouraged me to keep going and pointed me back to where my strength comes from: Christ. Thank you!

To all of my family and friends who have encouraged me along the way – either emotionally, financially, or otherwise – I sincerely thank you.

Part One

The Diva Deals

Chapter 1

I t came upon me without warning and for no apparent reason. But then it kept happening, time and again.

And I had no clue what it was or how to stop it.

In the two years since I had been declared free from a rare and usually fatal head and neck cancer, life had been good. Whenever we could, my husband Ellison and I travelled the hour-and-a-half north from our home in Tucson, AZ to Phoenix so we could visit our daughters Neema and Imani, see their families, and enjoy our two new grandbabies Jarek and Jaden as they grew into toddlers. I still saw my two friends and neighbors regularly, going to Debbie's house to get my nails done while Josie dropped in often for her coffee, my tea, and our chit-chat sessions, and there were phone calls with my friends in California and the East Coast. I attended church and worked with the worship team, but I kept my duties there to a minimum. I knew I needed to take it easy after battling cancer and found that I appreciated the lighter load from my previously heavy church responsibilities.

There was one stressor in my life: money. Ellison was unemployed and worked a variety of odd jobs, a photography gig here and a website design job there, to help us make ends meet. We were living off whatever he brought in and the grace of God; at times it was tough, but I was fine with that. He started to look for work in Phoenix, and since we were up there often to see the girls and their families anyway, we began thinking we'd eventually end up moving there. We found ourselves a new church home at a congregation we'd earlier encountered when we spoke at that church's Valentine's Day dinner for couples and started driving to Phoenix every weekend.

Life was busy—but life was good! I'd beaten cancer and my faith in the Lord was strong. As far as I was concerned, I was a happy woman. I was grateful—and content.

The weight loss that resulted from my time with cancer also gave birth to a beloved routine—Jazzercise, which I'd been attending for about a year. Classes took place three times each week, and each workout was fun and energizing. Every Friday session was capped off with a few of us going to Starbucks for coffee and conversation.

Ellison and I had one vehicle, and it was on one particular Friday morning that I drove myself to the Jazzercise studio with plans to come home in time for Ellison to then drop me off at the coffee shop before he took the car to run an errand. Jazzercise that morning was invigorating, and I let my muscles relax as I completed the five-minute journey home and parked the car.

As I walked inside, I heard Ellison in our bedroom—but was suddenly compelled to head straight toward our guest bedroom. It was an area of the house I used as my craft room but hadn't visited much since I had cancer. It was as though I was an automaton directed via remote control by an ambiguous master.

Without any thought as to what I was doing or why, I sat on the bed, reached down, unlaced my sneakers, and tossed them aside. Then, still wearing my exercise clothes, I crawled under the covers.

And I started to cry—a full-on, boo-hoo, snotty cry.

I stayed there no more than a couple of minutes, maybe three. Then, just as unknowingly as I had arrived, I got up from the bed, went into the bathroom, and cleaned my face. As I looked up from the sink and into the reflection of my own eyes in the mirror, they betrayed nothing. They were brown, a little bloodshot, and utterly unenlightened. Otherwise, I looked as fresh as when I had left the studio no more than ten minutes earlier.

I came out of the bedroom and walked over to the kitchen.

"I thought I heard you come in earlier," Ellison said. "Ready to go?"

"Yep. Let's go."

He had no idea what had happened. Frankly, neither did I.

So it was, on that Friday morning seven years ago, that I had my first encounter with depression. I didn't know that's what it was at the time, and I wouldn't realize it for another couple of weeks even though the sad episodes kept occurring every other day—just as unconsciously as the first and with just as much mystery. Most of the time, I'd wake up in the morning in an unexplainable, blasé funk. I'd be moody and down in the dumps, a far cry from how I'd always started each day in the past, happy and with purpose. I never needed an alarm to wake up, and I had my morning ritual of getting up, taking a shower, making my tea, and watching the morning news. But now I was dragging myself out of bed, forcing myself to get into the shower, and then slowly plodding to the kitchen as if I was sloshing uphill through four feet of sludge.

I had only one other boo-hoo session. I woke up one morning in a deeper funk than usual and the sludge felt more like quicksand. By the time I got to the couch with my tea, the tears came. Again, the cry lasted for only a few minutes, but it left me drained. It was everything I could do to tap the remote to turn on the TV.

I didn't say anything about how I was feeling to anyone, not even Ellison. What was I going to say when I had no idea what I was dealing with? I didn't pray about it, either—at least not specifically. Every once in a while, I did quietly query, "Lord, what's going on?" But that was it; physically I felt fine, and the episodes were brief, so I had no reason to suspect a major medical issue.

A couple of days after my second cry, I took a call from a longtime friend who lived in Illinois. Tanya was one of the many people I contacted when I was diagnosed with cancer, but she never called back for the longest time. When she did, she apologized and said the cancer was just too much for her to deal with at the time. I understood that. I knew that she had dealt with situational depression in the past and had seen deeper depression take place in her family. I guessed that she was simply dealing with something related to that at the same time I was getting my cancer treatments.

I didn't say anything about how I was feeling to anyone, not even Ellison. What was I going to say when I had no idea what I was dealing with?

Maybe it was my knowledge of her background that compelled me to say it.

"Guess what happened to me?"

I told her everything—from the first breakdown after Friday Jazzercise to that morning's funk. "I don't know what's going on," I concluded.

I wasn't expecting a response. It just felt good to tell someone.

"You know, you might have depression," she said. "You should talk to your doctor."

I heard her, and I respected her opinion because of what she had dealt with. But I didn't think that's what I was going through. I had no reason to be sad, no cause to be upset.

Still, I knew something wasn't right, and I already had an appointment set for the next day with Leslie, my primary care physician. I'd been seeing her regularly for routine check-ups, and after talking with Tanya, I decided I should mention my episodes and get her take on them.

I went in and told her about my peculiar boo-hoo and morning funk sessions and explained how they baffled me. Leslie then gave me a worksheet that posed a variety of questions about how I was feeling. I filled it out in about five minutes, and then patiently waited as she scanned my responses. Finally, she looked over at me.

"This is what's going on," she said matter-of-factly. "You're dealing with some depression."

There it was again. I didn't say anything in reply. I just started to cry.

Part of me was relieved to know what it was because not knowing was scary. But this was uncharted territory. *Now what's going to happen?* I wondered.

Leslie leaned over and gave me a hug. "We're gonna get you through this," she said. "You're going to be okay. I'm going to put you on a medication. It's a mood stabilizer, not heavy duty, and we'll start you out at a low dosage."

She told me about the medication, Citalopram, and called in the prescription. Then she said she wanted to see me again in a couple of weeks to see how I was doing. As I drove from Leslie's office to the pharmacy, I was having a hard time wrapping my head around it all. *Depression. I have depression? Okay. But why?* I didn't understand, but I did feel better knowing what it was and that I was going to get medication for it. But I also determined I wasn't going to tell my friends or anyone at church about it. *They'll think I'm going crazy,* I thought. I'd always believed someone who had to be medicated for depression was probably beginning to lose it—and I was all about keeping it together.

My family needed to know, though, and when I told Ellison that night, his first reaction was interesting—and confusing. "Now it makes sense," he said. I didn't say anything. I didn't know what made sense to him, or why it did. When I told the girls, both reacted in largely the same way they had when I told them I had cancer: Imani was clinical; Neema took it in stride.

After that, it wasn't mentioned again over the next two weeks, not even at the end of a day when I'd had another funk. The only person I spoke to about it was Tanya. We talked pretty much every day, and I told her what Leslie had diagnosed and prescribed. Tanya encouraged me to be sure to keep taking the medication and suggested several other things, such as exercising or changing my diet, that might help combat the depression. She was helpful and supportive—a welcome non-judgmental voice with whom I could talk freely about how I was feeling each day.

It's not that I feared I was going to be judged by Ellison and the girls—not consciously, anyway. I could easily imagine them thinking, "Oh, here we go. Something else is wrong with her," and I didn't want them to feel that way, especially after all they had gone through when I had cancer years earlier. None of them were trying to be judgmental about the depression, and they certainly never *said* anything critical, but I just felt they wouldn't understand it because I didn't understand it. Plus, I believed people in general were more sympathetic and understanding about a medical diagnosis like cancer. Depression, though, was something else, where others think, "Well, she's just in a bad mood. She'll get over it."

Leslie warned me that it would take some time for the medication to affect my system. By the time I went in for my follow up, I'd still experienced some funky mornings minus the boo-hoo sessions, and while they hadn't been as bad, they were still there. Leslie upped the Citalopram dosage to ten milligrams, and the episodes started to fade away. By the time summer arrived, I was more or less myself again.

That was a good thing, because I ended up moving from Tucson to Phoenix in July to help Imani and her husband Malik with their kids Amara and Jarek. Imani was working full-time and Malik had been home with the children that summer, but he was a teacher and headed back to work in the fall, day care

"Well, she's just in a bad mood. She'll get over it."

costs were ridiculous, and they didn't have enough money to cover it. Since we were already in Phoenix every weekend for family and church, Ellison and I decided that it would be best if I stayed up there, lived with them, and helped take care of the grandkids during the week. Then, when Ellison finally found work in Phoenix, we'd find a house, move from Tucson, and I'd keep taking care of the children in our new place.

I moved in with Imani and Malik the same weekend as Amara's third birthday party and settled in. I also assisted by doing the laundry, cleaning the house, and making sure the kids napped and the kitchen was ready in time for Imani to come home and cook dinner. I was essentially a full-time nanny and it was my pleasure. An added plus was that Neema lived just minutes away and was not working at the time because she was pregnant with her third child. I got to hang out with her and LaToya (her husband Keagan's daughter from before their marriage), Jace, and Jaden almost every day while Keagan was at work. Ellison stayed in Tucson to continue earning income through his odd jobs, but he visited us almost every weekend. I deepened my involvement at the church in Phoenix, too—becoming their administrator, singing with the worship team, and helping in women's ministry. Because the pastor and his wife had become friends with Ellison and me before we began serving on the leadership team, I believed I was going to be a good fit in my roles there. The pastor was funny, charming, and kind of charismatic, and our families had hung out together for cookouts or nights out for dinner before I began my administrative position. I anticipated thriving under his leadership.

For the next two years, I lived with Imani and Malik and it was easily the happiest I'd been since I had cancer. I was with my family every day—and Ellison and I weren't arguing. It was great for me, and I felt it was good for him because I was out of his hair. We had been arguing often, always about money at first, but then it usually deteriorated into him saying our tight finances were my fault because I didn't have a job. I'd reminded him that I didn't work because he had told me not to work so I could be available to the family and to do ministry with women. This deeper issue never came up any other time; it only presented itself when we argued, and we never took it any further than that. We just gave up and moved on. We definitely missed each other during this season apart, but we didn't miss the arguments.

Once Imani's children were preschool aged, I returned to Tucson in August 2012. I wasn't happy about it because I had expected to move to Phoenix to stay, but Ellison said he couldn't find work there—and that he felt God wanted us to stay in Tucson anyway. His discernment of God's voice was contradicted by our pastor in Phoenix who said God had told him we should take a leap of faith and move. I was disappointed with unrealized expectations about the move that didn't happen, struggled with resentment toward Ellison because I wasn't convinced he had done everything he could to find employment in Phoenix, and heartbroken to leave the girls and their families—especially the grandbabies.

But I consented—and hoped I could find another reason to be in Tucson apart from Ellison and my two beloved neighborhood friends, Josie and Debbie. A bit to my surprise, my depression remained under wraps. Sometimes I'd feel down, but it was minor, and my emotions stayed under control through the medication.

Less than a year later, I was back up in Phoenix—this time to move in with Neema and Keagan to help them with their kids while she became a student teacher. By then, Ari had been born, Jaden was three, and Neema and Keagan faced the same day care cost dilemma. I took up the same arrangement and roles as before, just in a different house, and I was more than happy to oblige. The difference this time was that I had no expectation that my stay in Phoenix was going to be permanent—though when Neema got a job upon graduation, Ellison and I agreed to have me stay six months longer until the end of the school year in May. Near the end of that period, Keagan got a job in California and left in April. On Memorial Day weekend 2014, Ellison and I helped move Neema and the children west to live with him and then came straight back home to Tucson.

After a combined three years of nanny work, I was more than ready for a rest.

There was another contributing reason for my exhaustion, though. Just before I had moved in with Neema and Keagan, things had started to change for me at our church in Phoenix. By then I'd learned that the pastor with whom I had strongly connected as a friend was quite a different person once I was on his staff. We butted heads often in my role as church administrator. I didn't feel he was a servant leader. He didn't seem to care about what was going on with us personally as staff. It appeared he was more concerned about what was happening in the lives of the church's attendees than with his own leaders. He and I had several conversations about this, but nothing ever changed. Slowly, I became more frustrated with him as my pastor—and therefore more disconnected. On top of that, each staff member went his or her own way as they served, a dynamic far different than I had ever experienced in my previous years of church work. While I was friends with two members of the staff, we were a bunch of individuals serving with each other but not alongside one another. I didn't feel like I was part of a team, and that was disheartening.

I was embarrassed that I was weeping, and angry that no one was acknowledging that.

Then came the Sunday when the pastor took the leadership staff out to lunch after service. There were about twelve of us around the table at a fancy restaurant, its atmosphere suitable for what I'm sure the pastor felt was going to be a happy, celebratory occasion. After we placed our orders, he asked us to go around the table and had everyone take turns sharing encouraging words about the team and how we felt about our service as leaders at the church.

One by one, people started telling how fulfilled they were and how their relationships with one another were strong and growing. I don't believe they were putting on but were expressing how they genuinely felt at that moment. Yet with each one I felt myself sinking deeper and deeper into a bottomless pit. I quickly became terrified for it to be my turn because I didn't know what I was going to say. I was embarrassed that I was weeping, and angry that no one was acknowledging that. I didn't feel like they did. At all. About anything. I didn't want to lie, but I also didn't want to be Debbie Downer.

When they finally got to me, I was bawling. "I don't have anything to say," I muttered, and excused myself to go to the bathroom, where I did everything I could to pull myself together. When I returned, I made it through the meal without another meltdown. No one asked me what was wrong or how I was feeling, including the pastor who was sitting directly across from me.

When we left, the pastor walked next to me, and he did ask me what was going on—with *Ellison*. He hadn't been to church for several weeks and wasn't at the luncheon. I knew why Ellison had been away, but I didn't think it was appropriate for me to reveal that reason. Besides, he was Ellison's pastor and Ellison was part of the leadership team; it was the pastor's responsibility to check on the well-being of others in his church.

"Maybe you should call him," I said in a quiet monotone. And then—perhaps because I hoped it might help me, maybe because I thought it might spark a reconnection between the two of us, I really don't know exactly—I told the pastor about my depression diagnosis. He was the first person outside of my family and Tanya that I decided to trust with this information, this *admission*. It was as though I had walked out onto the end of a pirate ship's plank.

"Oh really?" he said. "Did they give you medicine?"

That seems a weird question to ask, I thought. "Yes. It's Citalopram."

"Oh, that's lightweight stuff."

And that was it. That's all he said then, and all he ever said afterward.

What made it worse was that he had preached sermons where he said he had dealt with depression himself and had even previously worked in the mental health field. There are three people outside of your family that you should be able to share things with and feel a level of concern, care, and confidence: your doctor, your lawyer, and your pastor. As a Christian, it's obvious which one of the three is most valued.

I felt as if my pastor had come behind me and pushed me off the plank into shark-infested waters. He had failed me.

It was awful—and for the first time, I truly felt the stigma that I believe exists in the Christian church when it comes to depression and other mental illness.

That's why you don't tell people, even other Christians, I ruminated as I got into my car. *They either don't care, or they think you're crazy.* I was devastated—and that was the start of the end of my relationship with that pastor.

In a sad irony, my depression episodes returned. I had entire days where I was mired in a sad, sunken funk, so my Citalopram intake was increased. I continued serving at the church out of a sense of obligation, but I was miserable. I didn't feel appreciated and felt like anything I said was taken negatively or perceived incorrectly. I was made out to be the bad guy, and I didn't have anyone else to talk to about it. God hadn't released me yet to leave the church, so the one place where I could consistently turn for solace in the past—to worship, commune, and be uplifted, even in my worst days of depression—was no longer a comfort.

14

Then the situation at church worsened because of an internal issue unrelated to the staff lunch and discourse with my pastor. Within a few months, early in my yearlong stay with Neema and Keagan, Ellison and I finally left the church there to find a new one in Tucson. We were disappointed and wounded by what had transpired, and the depression episodes increased as I realized that nearly all of my non-family relationships and sense of purpose in my work were tied to church.

I found myself sitting in my house with nothing to do and no one to do it with. But we carried on—and the depression faded away as soon as we found a new church home in Tucson under Pastor Michael Lopez and his wife Maria, where I was soon singing worship and serving as his church administrator.

I also felt led by the Lord to write a book about my cancer experience. I met with an editor and publisher in the spring of 2014, and then spent much of the rest of that year in California helping Neema and Keagan with the grandkids after she became pregnant with her last child, Jabari. I did a bit more work on the book manuscript and started working weekly with my editor, Eugene, after returning to Tucson. *Cancer With Grace* was finished and published by the end of October 2015. I had a big book launch party at the house: Neema came in by herself from California and Imani came down from Phoenix with Amara and Jarek, while my cousin Stephanie came all the way from the East Coast to be part of the celebration. Also present were Eugene, Josie and Debbie, and Pastor Michael and Maria, with whom I had experienced much healing and restoration from the hurts of the previous church.

I was happy, with no depression flare-ups of any kind the previous two years. I was content as a mother, grandmother, and wife, with Ellison and I having received some counseling for our argumentative issues and doing well as a couple. I was thrilled to have the book after enjoying the writing process and excited to use it as a tool to tell my story to others, fulfilling what I knew God had called me to do.

Little did I know that the depression was about to return— and it wasn't going to be alone.

Chapter 2

In the first few months after the book launch, I spoke at a couple of churches, told my story, and sold a few hundred copies of *Cancer With Grace*. I had also heard from people who had either read the book or recommended it to others, sharing how engaging they felt my story was and how God had used it in their lives to inspire their faith. It was incredible and humbling.

When I got up to get ready for church that Sunday morning in February 2016, I didn't know why I felt sad. It was just like one of those funks from before, only worse. By the time I went to get my clothes on, I just lost it. I was standing in my closet, sobbing so hard my stomach hurt. Ellison woke up, found me, and embraced me in his arms. Normally, his comfort always made me feel better, but even his loving care wasn't enough at this moment. I recovered enough to go into the other room and sit down in front of the TV, but I just stared at the screen and felt like I was sinking, being pulled into a pit the depths of which was not unlike the one I'd felt years earlier at the pastor's leadership lunch.

Nevertheless, I forced myself to go to church. Gratefully, one of the songs Pastor Maria had chosen for us to sing in worship, "You Are" by Clint Brown, always led me to tears anyway, so when I wept while I sang everyone surely thought it was because of the song. They had no idea about my past depression, and that was fine with me. But it was clear; it was back again—and with a vengeance. I decided it was time to pay another visit to my doctor.

She asked me what was going on, and I told her everything. Ellison accompanied me to the appointment, allowing Leslie to get his added perspective on my depression resurgence. He said he thought I'd been oversensitive during the previous few months and irritable at times for no reason. His comments took me a bit by surprise; he hadn't mentioned either concern to me before. But as they talked, and I thought about it, I determined he was probably right. I just hadn't noticed it in my own behavior.

Leslie looked at us and listened. After a brief pause, she swiveled her chair toward me and said she was going to change my medication to Escitalopram, which she called a "cousin" to Citalopram, and add another one for anxiety called Buspirone. She was sober and unemotional as she shared the new diagnosis, but despite her practical demeanor I questioned within myself the need for the anxiety medication because I still thought I was just depressed and nothing else.

Then she added, just as no-nonsense, "I think you're also dealing with some PTSD."

"No, I don't think so," I responded in the same matter-of-fact tone. But my thoughts were racing. *Really? Is that all you can come up with? PTSD is something that happens to military people who went to Iraq or Afghanistan. But I haven't been to war.* As I was ruminating, Ellison said, "Now it makes sense." Those were the exact words he'd said years earlier when I told him about my depression diagnosis—and, like then, I was just as confused again as to why he'd say that. It certainly didn't make sense to me.

"I think it is," she insisted, "and might be related to your cancer battle."

18

"No," I repeated, dismissing her claim as easily as if she'd said I was sprouting a third arm. "I'm really great with the cancer. I wrote the book. I gave a copy to you."

"Yeah," she said, "and I read it, and you dealt with it when you were going through it. But there may be some emotional things that you still haven't worked through."

"Well, we'll see," I conceded, and she gave me a referral to a therapist who worked specifically with PTSD patients. I took it—but I'd already decided. *I'm not going to talk to anybody*, I thought as Ellison and I headed toward the car.

On the way to the pharmacy, I kept insisting to Ellison, "No. This isn't PTSD," repeating everything he'd already heard me say to Leslie, almost as though I was arguing out loud to convince myself I was right. He listened to my rant and every now and then said, "Okay," not as though he were shrugging me off, but making it clear that he wasn't going to discuss anything with me at this point. I was so deep in my denial declarations, it didn't even occur to me to ask him what he meant by his comment back in Leslie's office.

I started on the new medications and dug in my heels. I had already seen Leslie in late January for my annual physical, so when I went back to follow up with her on the blood work from that physical, Leslie scheduled some new lab tests for me. She then asked if I had seen the therapist yet.

"No, I haven't called her."

Leslie frowned and gave me a stony expression. "Well, you need to," she emphasized.

I went home and tried to suppress Leslie's exhortation. A few nights later, Ellison and I were sitting in the living room. I was on one couch, he was on the other sitting diagonally from me. He had still not questioned me about the first appointment with Leslie, and I hadn't talked to him about it, either. But it was a nice, quiet evening, and I guess I was finally ready to bring it up.

"I just don't know about going to see this therapist," I said. "I don't have PTSD."

His voice was gentle but firm. "How do you know?"

"Because I know me," I said resolutely. "I know it's not the cancer. I *know* what God did for me and through me. I'm good with the cancer."

He looked over at me and I saw the concern in his eyes. "Well, you know you," he said, "but you don't know PTSD."

That's when it clicked. *He's right. I don't know PTSD, but I do know something is going on.* His response also showed me that he'd been thinking about it, too, but didn't want to push. I appreciated that. "Yeah. Okay," I said. "I'll call in. I'll go and talk to her. We'll find out if it is PTSD. And if we find out that it's not, we'll deal with whatever it is." But even then, in the face of Ellison's loving wisdom, I still believed it wasn't PTSD.

I made the call. The therapist's name was Hazel, and the appointment was set for March 8. Her office was in her home in

"Well, you know you," he said, "but you don't know PTSD."

a separate room off to the right of her front door, and while it was not a large room, it was inviting. Shelves were filled with books, plaques adorned the walls, and a big comfy chair was waiting for me in front of her desk. It was all cozy and comfortable. I took my seat as she took hers behind the desk. Hazel was polite, easy to talk to, and I proceeded to tell her why I was there with a full overview of Leslie's thoughts, ending with my mantra that I didn't think she was right about the PTSD diagnosis because I was fine about the cancer. I then handed Hazel a copy of my book as if to settle any argument on the matter.

"Do you think the fact that I already feel it's not PTSD is going to have a negative impact on the therapy? Is that going to block me?" I asked.

She was professional and calm. "No, it won't," Hazel said. "But we are going to talk about past traumas, going all the way back to your childhood."

That was unexpected, but I thought, *Okay, I'm committed to whatever we need to do.* I wasn't resistant, but I also wasn't sure where she was going with that. She continued: "PTSD is caused by trauma. It can be *any* kind of trauma." Then she opened up to me about some of the things she'd been through, including being a recovered alcoholic herself. Her willing vulnerability set me at ease—and brought to mind something I hadn't thought about, much less said out loud, for years.

"Well, there are alcoholics in my family also. My dad was an alcoholic, and an abusive alcoholic toward my mom. He was an alcoholic all my life."

I could hardly believe those words had come out of my mouth, and it was all I shared. But it was enough. "That can cause trauma," Hazel said, "and because that hasn't been dealt with professionally, *you've* dealt with it just fine, and who you've become as a person was the result of dealing with the dysfunction of the family. It has helped shape who you are today." Then she added, "It can also create codependency." She handed me a stapled set of papers titled "What Does Codependency Really Mean" and encouraged me to read it later. Hazel then explained that codependency is a loss of self or a failure to develop a sense of self in the first place. As a result, she said, we rely on others to find an identity for ourselves. We have no inner reality, but only that which comes from outside ourselves. We can get addicted to that outer reality.

Nothing immediately jumped to mind that caused me to think, "That's me!" But I did nonetheless find myself resonating with that explanation. She then mentioned that dysfunctional families can birth different family roles that carry over to our adult lives. She gave me another stapled packet on that topic, and I scanned the four different roles. I decided I was definitely going to read both handouts when I got home. Then Hazel gestured toward a strange gizmo over in the corner of the office—a long rectangular bar with a series of flashing lights and a couple of paddles. She identified it as an EMDR machine.

"We're going to use EMDR, which is an acronym for Eye Movement Desensitization and Reprocessing." She was very businesslike. "EMDR is an evidence-based therapy that has become increasingly popular. It involves revisiting the traumas you wish to work on. As this has the potential to retraumatize, the protocol provides you with a safe place to go to prevent this from happening. We'll use this as I ask you to remember those traumas."

I looked right at her as though I was intently listening, and I did hear the words—but my gaze bore straight through her and into my suddenly doubtful mind. *I figured I was going to come here, sit on your couch, answer all of your questions, lay it all out, and then you'd tell me what I need to do,* I thought. *But EMDR? What?*

"There are also some coping skills you can use," she said, and told me about three of them. The first was a breathing exercise called "Four-Seven-Eight." You inhale four seconds, hold for seven, then exhale for eight. The second was called the "Butterfly Hug," where you cross your hands over your chest, lock your thumbs, and then lightly pat yourself like a butterfly's wings as it sits on a leaf. The last was "Grounding," a process of firmly placing your feet on the floor, feeling the support of your chair, and then imagining that you are a tree, with the roots coming from your feet and connecting with the healing energy and strength of the Earth.

She then leaned back in her chair. "Do you understand everything I just told you?"

"Yeah," I said. *But I'm not coming back,* I thought. *The breathing is okay; the hug is a little weird; the grounding is way too weird. And that flashy machine? That was just hooky-hooky. Nope. I'm not doing that. Besides, I don't have PTSD.*

But I really don't let anyone all the way in. I only let them in so far.

As we exchanged goodbyes, she said she was going on vacation, but to call in and set up an appointment for after her return. I went home with no intention whatsoever of calling back. But I was still curious about the information she'd given me. Ellison wasn't home yet, so I made a cup of tea, sat down on the couch, and looked first at the codependency packet. It listed out five questions—and after I read and answered each one of them to myself, I sunk into the cushions and took a deep breath.

I responded "yes" to all of them.

First was, "Do you try to control others to relieve your fears?" I almost laughed out loud. I am a control *freak.* I try to control my environment in whatever way I can. In my house, everything is in place, exactly where I want it to be. If someone moves it even slightly, I get irritated. I control people through what I share and what I don't share. I do this so that others view me as this great, wonderful person who is helpful and big-hearted. To some, I'm the over-the-top diva that has it all together. To others, especially young women, I'm the queen mother who is either the second mom, the big sister, or the confidant mentor. To many, I'm both rolled into one. But I really don't let anyone all the way in. I only let them in so far. I'm afraid to let them know who I really am; the little girl that saw her mother get beat by her drunk dad. The one that believes that if he's a bad person, then I'm bad, too, and therefore they will see me as a bad person.

Second question: "Do you allow others to control you because you fear their rejection, anger, neglect, and/or abuse?" Not so much with others, but in my family, I feel like I'm the low man on the totem pole. Nobody really gets me, and because I don't let people in, I feel as though I'm the bad guy all the time. Next one: "Do you change or adapt your behavior for others?" When I feel like I am being judged or will be judged, I'll back off and be quiet, refusing to express what I'm thinking or feeling. That's quite unlike my diva/queen mother persona.

I took a sip of tea and addressed the fourth question: "Do you avoid certain people to feel safe?" Strangely, I tend to avoid people like me, especially if they come off as being bullies. Then the final question almost made me choke on my Earl Grey. "Do you get your sense of value and worth through other people and their approval of you?" My eyelids grew hot. I looked over at the dining room table and thought back to the celebration dinner for *Cancer With Grace*. My daughter Imani gave me a gift and a card. It said, "I was waiting for you to finally do something." Like I'd never done anything of any worth all her life—that I never accomplished anything because I never worked outside of the home—so writing the book was the "something." Finally. She was not only an "A" student, but an athlete and an artist; my other daughter's life dream was to be an educator while my husband was the entrepreneur who could do anything. I'm proud of each one of them. But I was always Ellison's wife or Neema and Imani's mom. Never Jacki.

I leaned over to the Kleenex box, right in its spot where it was supposed to be and whisked out a tissue to wipe off my cheeks. *Okay—so I'm codependent. Clearly.*

I set that handout aside and grabbed the other one about dysfunctional family roles, almost afraid of what it was going to reveal. I started with "Responsible Child / Family Hero." It read, "This child takes over the parent role at a very young age, becoming very responsible and self-sufficient." I was the oldest of five. The next closest in age, my brother Gregory, was over a-year-and-a-half younger, and David was two years younger than him. The next brother, Terrence, was five years younger and my favorite. I was old enough to be more of a big sister to him than the others. Later, by the time my sister Michelle was born, I was thirteen—and while I liked having three brothers, I loved having a baby sister. My mother—I've always called her "Mommy," even until the day she passed away in April 2017—was nearing forty when she had Michelle, and whenever we went out, people usually assumed I was Michelle's mother and Mommy was her grandmother. When she'd cry at night, I'd get up and take care of her. One day after school I just moved Michelle's crib into my room.

The description continued, "This child is a good student, and parents look to this child to prove that they are good parents and good people." I was an excellent student, and while my alcoholic father, whom I similarly called "Daddy," was not a factor, I thought Mommy might've felt that way about me.

Then came the kicker. "As an adult, the family hero is rigid, controlling, and extremely judgmental, although perhaps subtle about it of others and secretly of themselves. They achieve success on the outside and get lots of positive attention, but are cut off from their inner emotional life, from their true self. They are compulsive and driven as adults, but deep inside feel inadequate or insecure. The family hero, because of their success in conforming to dysfunctional cultural definitions of what constitutes doing life right, is often the child in a family who as an adult has the hardest time even admitting that there is anything within themselves that needs to be healed."

I got up to pour myself another cup of tea because my mouth had suddenly gone dry. *It was me!* The diva/queen mother was all that on the outside, but Jacki was all that on the inside. I also knew that the first time I had ever personally embraced healing was when I had cancer, and because it was the "Big C," I had no choice. It was either accept God's declaration I was going to be physically healed or agree to die. But I realized that I had never even attempted to acknowledge that I had anything emotionally or spiritually inside of me that needed healing. I had been

a Christian since I could remember—yet the idea I could need inner healing was unknown to me.

I returned to the couch with my tea, and as I again picked up the packet, I noticed that I was trembling. I read the other three descriptions. "Acting Out Child / Scapegoat" was the child that the family feels ashamed of and the most emotionally honest child in the family. He or she acts out for attention with anger that

I realized that I had never even attempted to acknowledge that I had anything emotionally or spiritually inside of me that needed healing.

the family ignores. *That's my brother David, the middle child. If there was anything to do wrong, he was the one that did it.*

26

He did drugs, ended up in jail, and got kicked out of the house. He was later diagnosed with schizophrenia and still struggles today.

"Placatory, Mascot, or Caretaker" was the child that takes responsibility for the emotional well-being of the family and becomes the family's social director or clown, diverting the family's attention from the pain and anger. This child becomes an adult who is valued for their kind heart, generosity, and ability to listen to others. Their whole self-definition is centered on others and they don't know how to get their own needs met. They become adults who cannot receive love, only give it. They often have caseloads rather than friendships and can get involved in abusive relationships in order to save the other person. They go into the helping professions. *That's Terrence, my favorite. He was very funny, and he was also the pastor, called to the ministry when he was twelve years old. When Daddy was literally drunk and living out on the streets of New York, Terrence left Florida to rescue him. He tried to make sure everyone else was okay regardless of what he was going through. Terrence is gone now. He died of kidney disease.*

"The Adjustor or Lost Child" was the child that escapes by attempting to be invisible. They daydream, fantasize, read a lot of books, or watch a lot of TV. They deal with reality by withdrawing from it. They deny that they have any feelings and don't bother getting upset. These children grow up to be adults who find themselves unable to feel or who suffer very low self-esteem. *That's Michelle, my little sister. She doesn't even really remember Daddy because when Mommy moved the family to Florida, Michelle was only six. She's the one that if we're all together, she is going to be quiet because the rest of us are loud. If you talk to her, she'll answer, but if you don't, you won't even know she's there. The complete opposite of me. Almost fifty, she ended up being Mommy's caretaker by default.*

My other brother, Gregory, likely fit that category as well—but I was done ruminating about it all. My entire family was right there, on those pages. The whole dysfunctional bunch, with me leading the way. I was the oldest, after all.

It was too much, too fast. It was too real. *I'll either deal with it or I won't deal with it,* I decided, *and I probably won't deal with it because I don't know how to deal with it.*

That's when Ellison walked in the front door. He glanced over in my direction.

"How'd it go?" he asked of my trip to see the therapist.

"It was okay. A little weird."

He proceeded to his office without another word—and that was fine with me.

I had been taking my new medications for a month and was doing well with them. But then one day I went to the pharmacy to renew the prescriptions, only to be told the health insurance wouldn't let them do it. Confused, I returned home and told Ellison about it so he could look into it—but for whatever reason I never put it together that the denied refills meant that I would be off the medicine. I suppose I'd been doing so well that it never occurred to me that I'd miss them while the insurance snafu was solved. Gradually, somewhere between the first and second week without the medications, I started having those slow, funky days again. When I was taking care of my goddaughter Gabriella three days each week for my friend Julianna, I was okay because I had something to do and someone else on whom to focus my attention. But the rest of the time, I was home by myself except for evenings, and even then, Ellison usually had to take care of carryover work from school or other projects in his home office. When I was alone, my funks were deeper, and I didn't feel like I could talk to Ellison about it because we were having issues then about something or the other, I don't recall, so I didn't seek him out.

I also forgot to ask about what was happening with the insurance, because I quickly reached a place, I don't even really know how, where I thought, *I just can't take this anymore.*

I just said to myself, I want to go to sleep, and I'll be okay if I don't wake up.

I thought of suicide, but I didn't consider those thoughts to be suicidal. I wouldn't go that far in my mentality. Instead, I just said to myself, *I want to go to sleep, and I'll be okay if I don't wake up.* But I never consciously thought, "I want to commit suicide."

So it was that I next came up with a strategy, a methodology by which I could go on that forever sleep.

I had plenty of Lorazepam, a sedative that I first obtained from my doctor years earlier to help me relax and keep my cool whenever I had to fly on an aircraft. Every time, one of those pills knocked me out even before the plane took off—and staved off those times when that feeling of being too crowded in caused me to panic and hyperventilate. I didn't know much else about Lorazepam, but I knew it was potent. I gathered a pile of them and placed them on my nightstand. I then went throughout the house and collected all the little keys placed above the door sills that are used to unlock the room doors should they be locked from the inside. I took them and hid them away.

When it was time for bed, I'd close the bedroom door, lock it, and take a couple of Lorazepam, knowing Ellison was working in his office across the house. I'd start to get good and groggy, but then think, *No. I don't want the door locked*, and I'd get up to unlock it, lay back down, and then just as suddenly think, *No, I do want the door locked after all*, and get up again to take care of it. Finally, I'd go to sleep after getting up once more to unlock the door. If I woke up for some reason in the middle of the night, I'd take a couple more pills. My reasoning, I believed, was foolproof. *If I take enough pills, I won't wake up.* I never took a bunch of Lorazepam at a time, though, likely because my mind reasoned that *would* be committing suicide—but when the next morning arrived, I'd be angry that I was awake.

I repeated this cycle, night after night, for two weeks. Sometimes I was so out of it that I'd go into the bedroom, undress, and leave the clothes in a pile by the bedside—something I never do because I always meticulously put away my clothing. One evening after Ellison and I had an argument I was so upset that I actually called Hazel; I had a handful of Lorazepam in my hand and was poised to take them. She calmly asked me what was going on, I told her, and she said that if I felt I had to take the pills, she could have me placed into a psychiatric ward so I'd be somewhere safe. That frightened me because I recalled a friend whose daughter threatened suicide and had to stay in a facility like that for several weeks. Even if I had to stay somewhere for a day or two, I figured I'd then have no choice but to tell others about it, and that would prove to be too embarrassing. In the end, I relented and promised I wouldn't take the pills.

I don't know if Ellison ever saw the pile of pills. Because I had so many of them in my system, when he came home from work I'd either already be napping on the couch or would go to bed shortly after dinner. Since he was already in a funky mood with me, he either saw them and ignored them or didn't see them at all. One time during that two-week period Ellison did tell me, "You've been sleeping a lot lately. Is it because you're really tired, or is something else going on?" That was my chance to give a full confession, but instead I responded with, "I'm taking medicine to make myself sleep." He didn't get that I was doing it deliberately, and I certainly didn't tell him that's what I was doing, so he never thought to investigate it further. He also didn't know that I had stopped taking my other medications. He knew about the insurance snafu but did not know my meds had run out.

I'd been off my medications—and decidedly off my rocker—a full three weeks when it was time to see Leslie again, this time as a follow up session for the added lab tests. She came in and greeted me with a smile. "How are you doing?"

I'm alright," I said, but I must not have been terribly convincing. She cocked her head to the side and raised her eyebrows. She went to the exam room desk, sat down at the computer, called up my files, and began reviewing my lab results with me, indicating that all was well. Then, almost as if it were an afterthought, she asked, "And how are the new medications working?"

Here goes, I thought. "Well, they were doing fine, but I haven't had any in about three weeks because of a problem with the insurance."

Leslie's fingers froze on the keyboard and she looked at me, awareness flushing her face. "Oh!" she said. "So *that's* what's wrong with you." She leaned forward toward me. "You *cannot* just stop taking those."

I let out a breath. "I didn't just stop," I responded. "I couldn't get them," and I outlined what the insurance company had told me.

She rose, excused herself, and returned with her medical assistant. Together, the two of them got the insurance company and the pharmacy on the phone. Neither of them got anywhere, and Leslie was not happy about it at all. She left again and returned with what seemed like an armload of sample packages. By now, she was all in a tizzy. "I wanted to give these to you in the first place," she said, "but it would've been more expensive. Take two. Now."

Wow, I thought. *Am I that bad?* But I had my water bottle and went ahead and took the pills. Then she added, "You really need to see the therapist."

"I did have my first appointment," I told her, wondering how fast the meds I had just taken were going to take effect, "but she's been on vacation and I haven't called back."

"Well, make that appointment," Leslie said, "and tell me what's been happening since you've been off the medications."

"I've had some funks. Really deep ones," I offered, not sure how much I wanted to divulge.

"Did you have any suicidal thoughts?"

Well, there it is, I thought. "Yes."

"Did you have a plan?"

"Oh, yes. But it didn't work." Then I told her everything.

She listened carefully—but, after asking and confirming that I did not have a gun at home, did nothing else other than say

Wow, I thought. Am I that bad?

she wanted to see me again in a few weeks. By the time I got home, no more than a half hour later, I could already feel the effect of the samples. The edge was gone, as was the funk. I could think clearly again. When I told Ellison what Leslie had said about the medications, it was the first time he realized that I still didn't have them. He got on the phone again, solved the issue with the insurance company, and I finished off the samples before I finally got my refills of the original prescriptions a few days later. I briefly considered telling Ellison everything I had shared with Leslie, but I just couldn't bring myself to do it.

I was stable once more—and felt so good that I again thought that the second session with Hazel wasn't necessary. I had the info on co-dependency and dysfunctional family roles. I actually tried the breathing technique and found that it worked, but I wasn't going to do the weird butterfly hug or grounding stuff. I figured I was fine, so what was the point? Every now and then, though, the memory of Ellison's earlier exhortation, "You know you, but you don't know PTSD," replayed in my mind, and when I returned to Leslie to see how the renewed medications were doing, she again reminded me, insistent as ever, that I needed to set up the next therapy session. The combination of her voice and Ellison's finally won out, I made the call, and my second therapy session with Hazel was set.

Had I known then what was about to come, I probably wouldn't have returned. Because what was revealed was going to shock—and change—my life.

Chapter 3

T hree months after first seeing her, I walked back into Hazel's
office willing, and I believed mostly ready, to do whatever
was needed to figure out what was going on with me. As I took
my seat, I looked over at the EMDR machine and imagined the
glittering of the blinking lights. *Hooky-hooky or not, see this
thing through*, I told myself, *and let's get rid of this PTSD the-
ory for good.*

I settled into my chair, took a deep breath, and tried to allow
Hazel's reassuring smile to set me at ease. We got reacquainted
and I told her about all that had happened since our first visit,
including my phone call to her. Hazel didn't mention it or anything else specifically, but she allowed me to do all the talking. At
the end of my recap, I assured her, "Other than that, everything
is going fine. It's been a rough couple of months, but I'm doing
better."

"That's good to hear," Hazel said. She then slid a form
across her desk. "Before we get started, this is a consent form
for EMDR." She said she thought I was a good candidate for the
treatment and that she planned to use it with me in upcoming
sessions. I signed the form, trusting her expertise but still not
fully understanding why it was needed. As I gave it back to her,
she continued, "I also want you to come up with a 'safe place.'

Because EMDR brings back past traumas, and you're going to go through them again, after talking about them you need a safe place to go to where you are not experiencing the trauma. This safe place can be a real place from the past or present, or a pretend place in your mind. Either way, I want you to find one. I won't let you leave the office if you're feeling any type of anxiety or having any physical reactions to the traumas we talk about. If I did, you wouldn't be safe."

Whoa! I thought. *It's gonna get that deep?* It certainly wasn't what I expected, but I somehow knew I needed to stay with this process.

"Can you think of a safe place where you can go?" she asked.

I entered the theater of my mind and it immediately projected the ideal spot. It was a real one from my childhood. I was raised in an "A" frame home in a housing development north of New York City called Juniper Hill. The neighborhood was lush and tree-filled. Many people assumed people of significant means lived in the development, and a few did, but my family wasn't one of them. We weren't wealthy, but we weren't destitute, either. Our yard had bushes and flowers in front, and Daddy kept a vegetable garden out back. The house seemed gigantic back then. It had five bedrooms, two baths, and a full basement, and on the second floor tucked beneath the angled roof was my bedroom. It looked out onto the neighbor's backyard, so the view wasn't anything to brag about, but it let in enough light to keep my room bright and welcoming.

In my room, there was a small door—the only one in the entire house—that led into our attic. It wasn't a large attic, probably no bigger than a walk-in closet in most homes today, but it had lots of space as far as I was concerned. A few boxes were stored in it, but it was otherwise empty. I went into that attic often as a little girl and spent hours at a time playing with my dolls or having private tea parties all to myself. I couldn't stand upright in the space because of the angled roof, and it had no windows for light; it's only illumination was a single, naked bulb activated by a pull string. It's bare wood walls exuded a musty smell, and the climate of the space largely matched the outdoor temperature and humidity since our home had no central air or heat. But all of that only contributed to making it a special place, a secret, precious space that I coveted and where I always felt happy and secure. My brothers never came there; in fact, I don't think anyone in my family ever knew that I went in there. If I was playing in the attic and was required to come down for dinner, Mommy or one of my brothers always yelled to get my attention. They never actually came up into my room to get me.

That little door into the attic was the portal into my tiny, safe playhouse from my earlier years all the way into middle school. At that point, I started babysitting and then worked other jobs, beginning that awkward adolescent transition toward adulthood, and my attic hideaway lost its needfulness. But it never stopped being my spot—and now I realized I could still go there, sit down, and be happy, even if it was now located in the recesses of my mind. I looked at Hazel. *That's it. That'll be my safe place.*

It never stopped being my spot—and now I realized I could still go there, sit down, and be happy, even if it was now located in the recesses of my mind.

"I have one," I told her."

"Good," she said, smiling once more. "Then let's proceed. We're going to spend the next couple of sessions reviewing some family history. I'm going to ask you some general questions, starting with up

until you were twelve years of age. What do you remember about
your birth?"

I almost laughed out loud. *Uh, I don't remember anything
about the day I was born. Who does?* But the expression on her
face told me the question was serious. "I was told I was born feet
first," I said. It was all I could come up with for that one.

"Tell me about your ability to bond with your parents."

"I wasn't particularly close to either one," I responded. "I
wasn't nursed by my Mommy. I was given formula."

"Is there any history of addiction in your family?" Hazel
asked next.

"As I mentioned last time, my father was an alcoholic. I later
learned the alcoholism was on both sides of the family. Both of
my parent's siblings had problems, as did two of my brothers."

"Do you know of any history of mental illness in your family?" she asked.

I thought for a moment. "There was some on my Mommy's
side. My aunt had schizophrenia. I didn't know that's what it was
back then. No one ever talked about her being mentally ill, even
when she lived with us for a while. I remember wondering why
she was talking out loud to other people when it was obviously
just her. I was told, 'She just has company.'"

Even after those few questions, I was amazed at what I was
sharing, but wondered if I was giving Hazel the kind of responses
she needed. She seemed satisfied with my answers, though, so I
figured I was doing well.

"What were things like for you at school?" she asked.

"I was a good student. I loved being at school."

"Can you recall any particular traumas during this period of
your life?"

"Mommy and I butted heads," I said, "but our relationship

was fine, other than that she wasn't very affectionate. At all. I'd go to hug her, and I could feel her body just tense up every time."

"What about your father?" Hazel pressed in.

"He went to work Monday through Friday, sometimes for two jobs at a time, then on the weekends he was absent, sometimes physically but always emotionally," I said. "That's when he did his drinking, on the weekends. It was never done at home, and I never saw him drunk during the week. Just on the weekends."

Hazel didn't comment. She only listened to my responses and seemed to sense when I was going to share more.

"He'd go wherever he went, get drunk, and then everyone would be on pins and needles. We didn't know when he was coming home or what would happen when he did. During the week, he didn't have much to say to anyone about anything. Then on weekends he'd start an argument about anything. My parents fought a lot." Their confrontations were mostly verbal—they didn't seem to talk to each other at all aside from arguing—but there was physical abuse, too. One incident seared into my memory was when I was twelve. I was walking out of the living room and saw Mommy on her hands and knees in the kitchen. She was scrubbing the floor right in front of the refrigerator, and apparently Daddy wanted something to drink and could not wait. He kicked her in the fanny so hard it moved her sideways. Thankfully, it didn't cause her to fall. That would've been bad since she was six months pregnant with Michelle at the time.

Not once do I remember them saying "I love you" to one another. Or kiss. Or hold hands. There was just conflict. That was the norm for me and my siblings. Mommy just took it. She mouthed back sometimes, but she didn't do anything else to stop it. In fact, she always said, "Well, he's still your father, regardless of how he treats me."

A squeak interrupted my thoughts as Hazel shifted in her desk chair. "What were the major events of your life during your early childhood?"

"My three brothers were born: Gregory, David, and Terrence."

"Do you remember any specific stress reactions?" Hazel asked.

"Not really," I said. "I'd isolate myself when my parents fought."

Hazel didn't ask where. I figured she assumed that's when I went into my attic, which was indeed the case. "Did you have any medical issues as a child?"

"I found out around age nine that I was allergic to penicillin, and I had tonsillitis a lot. I had to get antibiotics, which was how we found out about the allergy. I ended up having my tonsils removed at age eighteen."

"Were there any family crises?"

"Only the ongoing fighting with my parents."

"Tell me more about your siblings. What was their birth order?"

"Gregory was the oldest after me, with David next. Terrence was the youngest brother and I was closest to him, He's now deceased," I said. "Michelle was born later and was the youngest of all of us."

"Were there any developmental issues?" Hazel asked.

"Do you mean with me—physically or mentally?" She nodded. "Nope," I said.

"What about your family relationships? How did everyone get along?"

"I told you about Mommy. Daddy was not involved with us. He mostly worked," I said. "As a family, we went on occasional outings, usually around the holidays." As I answered, I sensed we were nearing the end of the session. Already. The time seemed to have flown by.

"Were there other interpersonal relationships for you?"

"I made friends easily. I played with my brothers and other boys in the neighborhood. Other than playing with my dolls, I played football or something with the boys rather than girly things. I really was a tomboy." I said. "I had a couple of good friends in fourth grade who remained friends through high school."

Hazel leaned forward. "Very good, Jacki. I think we'll stop there for today. Next time, we'll pick up where we left off at age thirteen. How are you feeling?"

"Good." And I was, all things considered.

It felt good that I was finally able to talk to someone about my childhood and get it out.

Hazel and I parted, and on the thirty-minute ride home from her office I processed what had just happened. It felt good that I was finally able to talk to someone about my childhood and get it out. I'd never mentioned these things before to anyone. *Okay,* I mused. *If this is what it takes to get to what is going on with me, I don't mind talking about it, and I felt comfortable and safe.* I also believed there weren't going to be any judgments made about me because I trusted Hazel and now knew I could be honest with her, and therefore with myself. I hadn't held anything back.

But I also knew I didn't want to talk about it with anybody else, including Ellison. When he got home, I gave him a rundown of the topics Hazel had brought up as though I was reading from a list of bullet points. I gave no detail about my responses to her. Ellison's face scrunched up in a, "Well, that's interesting" expression, but he said nothing else. My report must've been sufficient for him, and I was glad nothing else was required. I didn't want any conflict about it, and felt it was important to keep the content of my sessions with Hazel all to myself. Several sessions later, I asked her if that was okay, and she affirmed that I didn't need to tell Ellison anything if I didn't want to.

By then, I surely didn't—because we had gone even deeper, revealing events that I didn't even realize were actual traumas that made the PTSD diagnosis I originally doubted all too accurate and real.

One week later, after exchanging pleasantries, the exchange with Hazel at her office continued, starting with my teenage years, thirteen through nineteen. "Tell me about any issues you had in school or college."

"I was popular. I didn't go to college. There were no issues that I can think of."

She asked the same question regarding work, and I had worked part-time at a grocery store and gave the same response. "What about any issues with your family during this time?"

"Everything remained the same as it was when I was a child," I said. "My little sister Michelle was born, and I was like a second mother to her. I was still closest to Terrence and continued to have issues with my parents. I moved out when I was eighteen, and then saw my parents and siblings one or two times a week. I wasn't close to my parents, especially Daddy."

"And your other interpersonal relationships?" Hazel queried.

"They were good. I was still friends with the two girls from fourth grade," I said, then added, "I got engaged to my first boyfriend right out of high school."

That wasn't Ellison, but Duane. He was my first love—a tall, big, linebacker-looking sort of guy, a gentle giant with a compassionate heart to match. We were in a rhythm and blues band together, playing covers and some original songs; I was a singer and he played bass. We were pretty good and performed at parties, clubs, and even recorded a 45-rpm single. Duane loved me to pieces; too much and in the weirdest way, as it would turn out.

Like the last session, Hazel didn't ask for such details, though, and carried on. She questioned me about work relationships (they were good) and medical issues (I reminded her of getting my tonsils removed), then returned to my family. I told her about how my entire family moved to Florida when Mommy, who worked at IBM, got a transfer. At least it was the plan for all of them to go. It turned out Daddy stayed behind in New York— and never joined her or my siblings down south. My parents never divorced, but they remained separated.

Hazel jotted down notes with each response. "Did you have any psychological issues?"

"I was depressed during my senior year in high school. At one time, I thought I was having a nervous breakdown." *Interesting,* I thought. *I'd never said that before. So I guess I was depressed in the past, huh?* "I actually graduated at age eighteen-and-a-half because of my birthday."

"Do you remember being stressed during this time?" she asked.

"About four months before my high school graduation, I had an argument with Mommy and I moved out," I said. "I moved in with my boyfriend's parents, and his mother helped me talk it out with her. I withdrew even more from my parents. Emotionally, I cried a lot." Duane's family took me in like a daughter – and when I left home I ended up living at his parent's house for over a year. Duane and I, though, had separate rooms because we were fiercely committed to staying abstinent before marriage. When I finally got an apartment on my own, Duane and I kept seeing each other—until one day when he just dropped off the face of the earth. I had no idea what happened; I didn't hear from him or see him, and he never returned my calls. Every time I asked his mother about him, she said he was off doing this or that. It was strange, and before long I just assumed he was done with me.

That's when I started seeing Ellison, a classmate of Duane's and someone I had known since he was a little boy. As kids, Ellison and I were just friends, and not even close ones. In high school, I started being attracted to him, and on a school field trip to Manhattan to see the play *Purlie* we sat next to each other on the bus and in the theater. But it was a few years later, on a bus trip with our church to Brooklyn, that we sat together on the return trip and started dating shortly afterward. Before long, we saw each other often and talked on the phone almost every day, and things progressed from friendship into much, much more. It was about a year after we started dating that I got pregnant by Ellison—and then, wouldn't you know it, less than a week after that, Duane called. Turned out all that time he was away in secret—building me a house! His family was even in on the secret. When I told him about Ellison and the pregnancy, he was devastated. Even today, he'll tell anyone that I will always be the one that got away.

Hazel then kept us probing into my young adult years through age thirty, focusing first on my continuing education. I told her that I went to business school. It was an all-women's school in Manhattan, and while traveling into the city by subway was a little scary at first, the school was located adjacent to Grand Central Station which made it easier. From there, I went to work for a year at General Foods as an administrative assistant before being hired at IBM on my second try applying there.

"What happened now in your relationship with your spouse?"

"We had our first girl, Imani, got married to Ellison by a justice of the peace when she was ten months old, and moved to California for a new job, all in the same week." By then, Ellison and I were both working for IBM but in two separate divisions and buildings. He got the transfer to California, and I put in for my own transfer. We ended up in a similar situation out west with me in one IBM facility and him in another. "So it was a new job, a new environment, and a new baby."

"Did you have any trauma during this time?" Hazel asked.

"Before we were married, Ellison had a child with another woman. A boy. When we got engaged, the pastor at our church, my uncle, wouldn't consent to marry us because we'd had sex outside of marriage and he felt our marriage wouldn't work. That's why we got the Justice of the Peace. After moving to California, we started having some marital issues and we were separated for a few days." Then I added, almost as an afterthought, "And years later, of course, was the big earthquake." That was in 1989. I can still remember being in the laundry room of our apartment, feeling the tremor, and looking out into the parking lot to see the cars rippling like a wave.

I tried to keep my answers simple and direct, discerning that's what Hazel wanted.

It was frightening. There was damage in our place. It's amazing none of us were hurt or killed.

"What were your stress reactions?"

"Physically I withdrew. I was angry with Ellison." Again, I tried to keep my answers simple and direct, discerning that's what Hazel wanted. Plus, I knew we were getting close to the end of the session.

"Any other major events up until age thirty?" Hazel questioned.

"We had our second baby, Neema, and Ellison left me again. This time, he was gone for about a year."

We concluded and, like after the last session, I felt good about it all and gave Ellison a brief report that, again, seemed satisfactory to him. One week later, I was back—and Hazel picked us up where we left off from age thirty onward, starting with my relationships with Ellison, the girls, and others at work or at church.

"Our marriage was rocky for the first ten years. I felt like I wasn't as present emotionally with Imani and Neema because of my marriage issues, and I often felt ganged up on by Ellison and the girls," I told Hazel. "My other relationships were good, and I had a lot of friends."

"What about medical issues?" she asked.

"High blood pressure, high cholesterol, diabetes, cancer, and thyroid issues." I listed them off and thought humorously, *Other than that, I was great!* She asked if there were any psychological issues, and I mentioned the depression and anxiety. As stress reactions, I told her I isolated physically and became angry or sad emotionally.

"What would you identify as the major events?"

"My favorite brother died, my father died, and both girls got married and grandchildren were born." I also included my cancer experience and told her about leaving the church in Phoenix. To wrap up the history taking, she asked me to again state why I came in for therapy. "I had those unexpected meltdowns, and my doctor Leslie suggested I had PTSD."

At that point Hazel transitioned our discussion, asking me to go back through each of those age periods and identify specific events that caused any kind of trauma for me. As we talked I came up with five: my dysfunctional family life, my lack of relationship with Ellison's son, my relationship with my father, my mother not bonding with the children, and my marriage. I was surprised these were considered traumas because as far as I was concerned, they were just part of what my life was. She then asked for a "target memory" for each one, and to pinpoint a negative and positive belief. They were:

- Dysfunctional family life—when I left home. My negative belief was, "I can't do anything right," and my positive belief was, "I am a good person." I added to this one the time I went to juvenile hall. My negative belief was, "I am undeserving of love," and the positive was, "I am lovable and a capable person."
- Relationship with my father—my father passed out in the car in the driveway. My negative belief was, "I'm not a good person because Daddy's not a good person," and the positive was, "I am good."
- My mother not bonding with the children—my high school graduation. My negative belief was, "I'm not appreciated," and the positive was, "My efforts deserve acknowledgment and appreciation."
- My marriage—two memories. My negative belief for one was, "I'm not good enough," and the positive was, "I am good enough." My negative belief for the other was, "I am not important to Ellison," with the positive being, "I am important."

With that accomplished, we were done—and Hazel told me that next time, we were going to begin using EMDR. After all I had revealed and learned, I was strangely ready for the process

I first thought was hooky-hooky. I knew what had happened thus far had helped me and figured that what was still to come was going to have the same outcome.

It did.

But it sure wasn't easy.

Chapter 4

When Ellison arrived home that evening, he asked how things went—but this time my overview wasn't enough. He wanted to know more.

"You know," I said softly and evenly, "I don't want to tell you what we talked about anymore. It's something I want to keep to myself. I don't want to keep revisiting it." I explained that when I "put away" the things I discussed with Hazel—which I did each time while picturing a little Tupperware bowl being hermetically sealed—talking to him about them meant taking the things out again.

Ellison was quiet, uncomfortably so. He wasn't upset, but I could also tell he wasn't happy. "What are you thinking?" I asked.

"I just feel uncomfortable with you talking to someone about things that have happened to you that I don't know about," he said.

I appreciated the candor in his response, but also knew I had to be just as frank. "Well, you're just going to have to deal with it." By then, I knew I was going to be writing this book, and added, "When you read the book, you'll find out."

I couldn't understand then why it made such a difference to him that I was talking to someone else about things he didn't know about. *We've been married for over thirty years*, I thought, *and you've never known any of this stuff. You never thought to ask about it, either.* Now I think his view was ego driven because he was unsettled with how what I said was going to make him look to others. My daughters have since shared that they were more troubled about learning exactly what I went through. That's why I've chosen to change all the names used in this book except for my own, to honor their concerns about perception yet still tell my story unabridged and fully intact.

When I arrived at Hazel's office the following week, we jumped right in with her asking me to tell her the first target memory associated with my dysfunctional family life: leaving home.

"When I had my tonsils out, I was eighteen and I was home recuperating. Duane came over to visit and Mommy made a vanilla milkshake to soothe my throat. But I didn't want it. That's when an argument started over the milkshake, and for some reason it was then I decided, 'You know what? I'm done with this. I'm not gonna do this anymore!'" I said. "I asked Duane if he'd get me out of there. I still had my little suitcase out from the three-day hospital stay. I packed it, Duane took me, and when we got in the car, I said, 'Just take me to your house.' That's when I talked to his mother about how I felt."

"What is your negative belief about yourself related to this incident?" Hazel asked.

"That I can't do anything right."

"And your positive belief—the one you want to get to?"

"That I'm a good person."

She got up from her desk. "On a scale of one to ten, where would you rank the negative belief?"

It didn't take me long to respond, "Eight," and right away Hazel was next to me with the EMDR machine in tow. She first disinfected the small paddles, each one no larger than a new car key remote that then fit them snugly into the palms of my hands. She then started the lights on the machine, and I noticed they went left to right, back and forth, and that the paddles vibrated in sync with the movement of the lights. *Bzzz, bzzz. Bzzz, bzzz.* Hazel told me to follow the lights with my eyes, and she adjusted the speed until it was comfortable for me to follow.

"Now watch the lights—and go back to that incident," she directed. "Relive it in your mind."

So my eyes monitored the lights as though I was tracking a hypnotist's watch and I entered the scene from long ago—feeling the soreness of my throat and the angst as the milkshake was offered. Hearing the frustration in Mommy's voice and the anger in mine as I made my declaration. Smelling the familiarity of my room as I loaded my suitcase and the exhaust of Duane's car as we drove away. I made it all as real as I could—and I must've felt it, too, because when Hazel stopped the machine no more than a couple of minutes later, I was weeping.

"Take a deep breath," Hazel said, "and tell me whatever comes to you."

I don't remember what I said, but I do recall apologizing for crying.

"You don't have to apologize. What's making you cry?"

Again, my response alludes me, but I did think, *This seems so trivial—that an argument over a milkshake would cause me to leave home.* I also considered, *I've never told anybody about this other than Duane's mom. I never told Ellison about this. But I now realize how that one incident changed where my life was going to go from that point on.*

"Okay," Hazel said. "Let's go back." She started the machine, I followed the lights, and I reimagined the same memory until the lights were stopped and I relayed how I felt. We repeated this process over and again—until I got tired and didn't have anything else to say. But Hazel wouldn't let me drop it. In fact,

we continued working on that memory into a second session the next week.

Finally, after about twelve trips back and forth in my mind, I progressed to the point where my positive belief was a ten and my negative belief—well, it was gone. As though it never existed.

EMDR wasn't hooky-hooky. It worked. It was weird, but it actually worked.

EMDR wasn't hooky-hooky. It worked. It was weird, but it actually worked. And the fact that I don't recall my responses to Hazel to this day is a testament to the effectiveness of the EMR treatment. I can talk about it now because I don't remember what I said and it's no longer traumatic.

I journeyed into the next memory about one-third of the way into that same session. In it, I was fourteen and woke up one spring Saturday morning and started doing my weekly chores. I was dusting the living room when Mommy came in from the kitchen in a huff.

"Get dressed," she said. "We're going out."

It was so abrupt she didn't even give me a chance to ask why we were departing or where we were going. Her tone indicated that I better not ask, even if it was my tendency then to question and even mouth off at many things she said. Clothes on, we marched to the car, and without another word drove down the hill, into town—and straight into the parking lot of juvenile hall.

I knew what the place was. But I had no idea what we were

doing there. We walked up to the front desk, and it reminded me of what I'd seen on TV when characters walked into a police station. The counter was tall and the person behind it looked stern.

"Her behavior is too much for me to handle," Mommy said without even a glance in my direction. "She belongs here."

I felt out of place, confused, and a little afraid. Sure, I sassed her, but I never got into trouble. I was a good kid. Or so I thought. Yet here I was at juvenile hall, and Mommy wanted them to *keep* me.

A few minutes later, I was escorted by a social worker into her office. I had no idea where Mommy went. The room was orderly and even inviting, with knick-knacks all about the room and two chairs in front of a desk. I took a seat in one of them. The social worker sat down behind her desk and we conversed. I don't remember exactly what was said until the end. "You need to get your attitude together," she said. "You don't come from a bad family. You're not doing drugs. You don't have bad friends. Juvenile hall is not the place you need to be."

In all, I was there no longer than an hour and I was back home in plenty of time for lunch. On the drive home, Mommy said nothing and neither did I. I was relieved I didn't have to stay at juvenile hall, but I was also wondering what would happen if I really ended up doing something wrong in the future. Would I go to jail? Or worse? I was terrified, and I didn't know if Daddy or any of my siblings even knew if we'd been gone, much less what had happened. But we got home, I returned to my chores, and before long, my fears subsided. Life went on, and I was less mouthy— for a while. But I eventually resumed back-talking every now and then. I often had something to say about everything.

I came out of the memory and don't recall my conversation with Hazel, but my negative belief of being undeserving of love quickly went away through the EMDR process, fully replaced by the knowledge that I was a loving and capable person. That allowed us to go right into the next memory. It took me to a night just three years later.

It was cool but not cold even though it was close to my midnight curfew, and Duane had just brought me home from a date. We parked at the curb and began walking up my driveway because he always gentlemanly escorted me to the door. We didn't have a garage, so Mommy's car was parked closest to the house with Daddy's right behind it. I noticed he was there, outside, sitting in the front seat of his car, and as we got closer, I saw that the front door was ajar. We went over—and Daddy was sitting up straight, his head slumped down onto his chest.

He was passed out drunk. Mucus was dripping from his nose.

Totally embarrassed, I didn't say a word. It was the first time Duane had ever seen him like that.

We kept walking to the back door. Duane politely gave me a kiss, said good night, and I went inside. I don't know what Duane thought, nor do I know if he did anything else before getting back in his car to drive off. I didn't know what to do, either, but I do know what I thought.

Well, that's my Dad. If he's that bad of a person, then I must be a bad person, too.

I took that negative belief with me as I went straight to my room, changed into my pajamas, got into my bed, and closed my eyes. There was no worrying if Daddy was okay and it never occurred to me that something else, like a heart attack, might have happened to him. I assumed he was drunk, simple as that. It had happened plenty of times before. Why lose sleep over it?

Now, all these years later, I confronted that negative belief through EMDR, and first told Hazel, "I'm ashamed of my father."

But by the end of that session, no more than fifteen minutes later, not only was my negative belief gone and replaced by the positive, "I am good"—but I was positioned, in the days that followed, to reconcile myself that Daddy was an alcoholic. He had a disease. His behavior was not my fault or my problem. I was able to free myself from how his drinking had held me hostage for so long.

I realized, too, that Daddy likely never knew what he put his family through because of his alcoholism. How wounded we were feeling and how broken we became because of his behavioral choices. It made me think back to another memory, years later than my date night with Duane but years before I reconciled myself with his disease. Ellison and I were married and in California, our girls both pre-teenagers. I received a call from my brother Terrence that Daddy had been in a car accident in New Jersey. It was bad, and he had to be helicoptered to the hospital and twice revived from near-death, once in flight and again on the operating table.

He ended up being in the hospital for six months, four of those in ICU. Early in the half-year period, I stood up in church and asked everyone to pray for him. People all around turned and looked at me like I was crazy. Their faces all asked the same question.

I was positioned, in the days that followed, to reconcile myself that Daddy was an alcoholic.

"What father?"

I had never talked to them, to anyone in that church or any other before it, about him. They knew about Mommy and my siblings. But not Daddy. They just assumed he must've been dead long ago.

It was as though I'd made him non-existent.

Their reaction aside, I was emotionless when I made the

prayer request. I neither felt sad nor anxious nor—well, anything. It was as though I was speaking of a stranger.

For the next several days, that bothered me. How could I not feel anything at all for my father lying in a hospital on the verge of dying? That's when I told myself, *You know what, Jacki? He's still your father. You're the one claiming to be living for the Lord. You should have some kind of compassion—some, anything, for this man.* So I made myself call the hospital every day, twice a day. Even though he was in a drug-induced coma, I made the calls to his nurses and closed each one with this final statement: "Tell him his daughter Jacki called, and that I love him."

We had never said those words to each other. No one in my family growing up had said those words to one another.

It was during that time that I believe God started dealing with me about my perception of Daddy. It made a difference, too—because several years later he developed prostate cancer. I was the only one he told, and he made me his medical proxy. After that, I called him about every other week for several years. Each call lasted all of five minutes because he never had much to say. He loved baseball, so if I asked him about that, he had a little more to talk about. That was the extent of our relationship but that was better than it ever had been. He died in 1998 from the cancer after it returned following remission.

Still, it wasn't until the successful EMDR that I was able to rectify myself with the effects of his alcoholism and let it all go. On the way home from that session with Hazel, I remembered back to when Daddy died. Because he didn't belong to a church, there wasn't a go-to pastor to perform the funeral service. In the end, one of Ellison's brothers who Daddy had known from childhood officiated the service. It was held at the funeral home and attendance was light. Daddy didn't have many friends and he had outlived most of his siblings. A few of them were there, along with the rest of us from the family.

Daddy's funeral was strange for several reasons. Only Terrence and I had renewed a relationship of any kind with Daddy. The rest of my siblings were estranged from him. Mommy hadn't contacted him since they were separated but never divorced, a span lasting over twenty years, yet she cried at the funeral. I recalled being shocked by that. As for me, I didn't have any regrets upon his death. I didn't feel I should've loved him more or wished I had apologized to him for this or that. I was at rest with his passing. Another weird thing was that we, as a family, were together in one place. That hadn't happened since I had left New York. I had seen Mommy, Terrence, and Michelle at least once a year because they usually came out to California for Christmas or other occasions, but I hadn't seen the other brothers for eighteen years. Finally, the norm in our culture was for the church presiding over the funeral to prepare and host a huge meal for the family afterward, but this funeral had no church. My sister-in-law ended up driving to KFC to pick up food for us. Such an ending for a funeral was unheard of.

By the time I got home from the session and in the days that followed before the next one, it was amazing to think through all of this and to come out at the end knowing with certainty that I was good with everything. I was okay with my Daddy.

The next session with Hazel started with me returning to my high school graduation. By now, I had stopped using the lights on the EMDR apparatus because they were giving me headaches. I still used the paddles, though, and simply closed my eyes as I journeyed back into the past. Graduation took place four months after I had left home to move in with Duane's parents and was held indoors in the school gymnasium. It was a warm day in June, and as I put on my cap and gown in the locker room in preparation to take my seat in the auditorium, I was excited and relieved.

The previous six months had been a challenge. Not only was I away from home, but I had a part-time job and had to work extra hard to graduate on time. Yet I did it and with excellent grades. I was proud of myself—and imagined how Mommy would feel. After all, I was the first of her children to graduate high school, and she had graduated high school as valedictorian of her class. While Daddy wasn't there, Mommy and all my other siblings were. When Pomp and Circumstance played, and I marched onto the gym floor and was given that diploma, it was everything I could do to keep my emotions in check.

I still used the paddles, though, and simply closed my eyes as I journeyed back into the past.

But Mommy didn't seem either excited or proud. It was almost as though she was disinterested. I watched other families around me smiling, taking photos, and handing out balloons or flowers to their graduate, but I didn't get any of that. Nor was there a party afterward. There was no celebration of any kind for my achievement—other than my gift: an electric typewriter. It was a practical gift since I was going on to business school and needed a typewriter, but there certainly wasn't a lot off sentiment behind it. In fact, Mommy wasn't overly impressed that I could become a secretary. She saw that as a lesser profession compared to hers as a technical writer at IBM.

Duane took me out to eat after the ceremony. He did everything he could to celebrate my achievement, and his parents also expressed their excitement for me. That made me feel good, but it also made me sad because I wasn't receiving the same type of recognition from my own family. The entire experience was bittersweet.

My negative thought was "I'm not appreciated," but after about fifteen minutes of EMDR, that thought was vanquished and replaced entirely with the positive thought that "my efforts deserve acknowledgment and appreciation." I don't remember any conversation with Hazel other than revisiting the memory a few more times before it was over.

Again, EMDR had done its remarkable work. The therapy was working.

Now it was time to deal with my marriage—and things were about to get truly hooky-hooky.

Chapter 5

As it turned out, EMDR was not used in my next session with Hazel. I didn't know that would be the case going in. But once we started our opening conversation, it was clear to her that I had a lot to say—that needed to be said—about my marriage before I could start working on the specific memories.

Ellison and I grew up together. Our parents were friends long before either one of us was born. We were around each other as small children, went to the same church, and attended the same schools. After the church bus trip as young adults that led us to start dating, we saw each other often: at Friday TV nights at my little studio apartment after church choir rehearsals, at Saturday dinner and movie dates, and at Sunday dinners at his parent's home after watching afternoon football games. By all rights we were a boyfriend/girlfriend couple, but we didn't have our first kiss for nearly a year. It finally came at the end of one of those dinner and date nights inside my door.

It was a great kiss—tender, deep, and all I'd ever dreamed it to be—and we had others. What we didn't have, though, was sex. It wasn't because of a religious commitment to celibacy before marriage, nor was it because I didn't give him the chance to go further. It just didn't happen until a couple of months after that first kiss, and I was okay with that. I was with Ellison. That was all that mattered.

Ellison and I were both working for IBM then, he as a research and development computer science technician in the Yorktown, New York plant, and me as an administrative assistant at the headquarters complex in nearby Armonk. One night when we were on a date, he needed to give a coworker a ride, I don't remember to where. When we picked the person up, she walked up to my side of the car, and instead of getting into the back seat, she opened up the passenger door and slid in right next to me. There was plenty of room because there were no bucket seats in the front of Ellison's 1976 Ford Thunderbird, and the fact that she got in the front with me and my boyfriend seemed, well, kinda weird. But I just chit-chatted with her until she was dropped off. I never thought any more of it.

Then, several months later, Ellison called me at my desk. He said he needed to talk to me about something important. His voice sounded solemn, quite unlike him. It made me nervous. We made plans for him to come by my apartment after work. When he arrived, I met him at the door. I'd never seen him look the way he did. I thought someone had died.

We sat down next to each other on the couch. Our legs were not touching, and he did not take my hand or otherwise initiate contact. "I have to tell you something," he said, looking directly at me. "I'm going to be a father."

"Oh. Congratulations!" My response wasn't sarcastic. It was upbeat, happy even, as though I was responding to him getting a promotion at work. I said it without even thinking. I was totally oblivious at that moment to the reality of what he'd just said.

He continued, "I want you to know that I don't plan to

continue my relationship with the baby's mother. But I am going to take care of the baby."

It all started to come together in my head. *Baby? Mother? Oh God.* It's bad enough, even though he never explicitly *said* it, to find out there's another girl, but to also find out that he's having sex with her and there's a baby on the way? I suddenly felt warm and my stomach fluttered.

"I really want to be with you," Ellison went on, "but I will understand if you don't want to be with me." Then he reiterated that his part in the child's life will be to take care of it.

I tried to sort it all out. *I want to be with him, and since he said he wants to be with me, that means the baby's mother is going to be out of the picture. He just wants to take care of the child financially. Right?* "I want to continue being with you," I said, straightforward and almost emotionless. It was all happening too fast.

Then, just like that, he got up to leave. I thought he'd want to stay or at least go out to get something to eat together after such a revelation. But no—he'd delivered the news, short and sweet, like he'd just reported an FYI to his day, and was done. Not knowing what else to do, I got up, too, and walked behind him to the door.

"Good night," he said.

There was no hug. No kiss. No anything. I couldn't focus. "Good night," I responded. My voice sounded small, almost non-existent.

The door closed—and something exploded within me. I leaned with my back against the wall, slid down to the floor, and wept. I couldn't stop for the longest time. Hot tears flowed, like lava pouring out from my shattered heart.

Later, I'd find out who the girl was. Actually, it was more that I figured it out. Ellison and I saw each other a lot. We were pretty much in the same circles and around the same people. Among those, I was pretty much the only girl around his age, and I knew there wasn't a lot of time or opportunity for him to see anybody else. Who could it be if it was somebody I didn't know? Looking back now, I honestly believe God, by His Holy Spirit, put her face in my mind. When I finally asked him if it was her, he said it was. I'd only seen her that one time. Otherwise, he never talked about her, and I didn't know her at all.

It was the coworker. The same one I shared the front seat with.

The baby ended up being a boy. Ellison's only son.

Hazel leaned back in her chair, taking in the account I'd just shared for the first time with anyone—and understanding how Ellison and I were dating and celibate when I found out about the child. She said, "So he cheated on you."

Whether I had been naïve or in denial, I don't know, but I now accepted the truth.

It was a statement, not a question, and it stunned me. I had harbored resentment toward Ellison over the years because he had sex with someone else before me. But I suddenly realized I had never reconciled myself to the idea, the *fact*, that Ellison had indeed cheated on me. He wasn't my husband then, but that didn't change the reality of the betrayal. I said nothing. I was embarrassed. Whether I had been naïve or in denial, I don't know, but I now accepted the truth. *Yes. He did cheat.*

I took a deep breath and continued the story for Hazel. It was a couple of months before the baby was born that Ellison and I started having sex, and I became pregnant with Neema just two months after his birth. By then, I understood that my assumptions about Ellison's financial-only role with his son were dead wrong. Yes, he and the mother, I assume, agreed to a monthly monetary amount, and he paid it like clockwork despite never having an official court order for the support. But not only was Ellison present at the baby's birth, but he had started spending time with his child, too, about every other weekend. And, of course, the more time he spent with the baby, the more time he spent with the baby's mother—and the less time he spent with me. Even worse, when Ellison was alone with the baby, he wouldn't let me join them. He felt that it was an already difficult situation and wanted to keep everybody separated. If everyone was separated, he reasoned, they'd be happy.

Maybe his son's mother was, but I wasn't. I felt very isolated from it all. Very alone.

And it stayed that way—though after Neema was born I focused on her, and Ellison was an active part of our lives, but I still had a sense of seclusion from him and his son that I simply pushed down and buried within me. He and I never talked about the issue. It just never came up. Ten months after Neema's birth, Ellison and I got married, and as his wife, I felt I should no longer be kept in the dark about his relationship with his son and thought Ellison would even take the responsibility to foster that relationship between me and his son. But again, my assumption was unfounded: I never got to be part of his son's life.

That didn't change until the son was eight years old—when I decided to contact the mother and arrange to have him come from New York to California to see Ellison for Father's Day. I love surprises and I wanted to do something extra special for Ellison that year, and the idea of having his son visit just popped into mind. I wasn't at all sure how his mother would respond and mostly, I expected her to refuse. After all, it was a long cross-country trip for one so young to take to a place—and other than Ellison, to people—he didn't even know. I called the mother at her work number, which I had access to because we were all working for IBM. It was the first time I'd spoken to her since that awkward night in Ellison's car.

When she answered, her nervous "Hi" gave away her reaction to hearing from me, but our conversation was cordial, brief, and to my astonishment, she consented to the trip. She also agreed with my suggestion (a shock to me as well as I didn't think it through in advance) that he stay with us for the entire summer. I told her I'd pay for everything, and after hanging up I made the airline reservations and emailed her the details.

When he arrived the Friday before Father's Day weekend, the girls and I met him at the airport. Neema and Imani were four and seven and were excited to be meeting their big brother. Because he'd never met any of us before, the son was understandably skittish, but I tried to just swoop him in to feel as much a part of our lives as possible. We drove straight to a restaurant across the street from Ellison's plant in San Jose, where I'd already made advance arrangements with the manager to help me spring the surprise on my husband. Ellison met me and the girls there for what he was told was a special lunch to celebrate Father's Day.

When we were seated, I announced, "We have one more gift for you," and the manager brought out his son. I don't think Ellison recognized him at first, but as the son walked closer, Ellison's eyes widened and lit up. He gave his son a hug, the girls smiled, and I sat back and exulted within. *Well done, Jacki.* I thought. *Ellison is flabbergasted—and really happy.* He kept hugging his son and then holding him away, saying dumbfoundedly, "What are you doing here?"

Ellison's son stayed with us through the end of August, over two months in all, and I thought the visit went well. We didn't travel anywhere special but did things in and around town, and we included him in our regular routine at home and at church. He played a lot with the girls, and the three of them played even more with Ellison when he was home from work. I gave him some chores and while he wasn't as responsible as the girls, there were never any problems. I presumed he was having a good time because he never asked to go home early. I also assume he talked to his mother when alone with Ellison, but I was never there for any of the calls. Truth is, for the entire stay I was treated by him as nothing more than a facilitator for his interaction with everyone else. It was hard trying to be a part of this person's life because I didn't know if he really wanted me to be a part of his.

At Ellison's initiation, his son returned two years later for Christmas. Though he never told me so himself, I imagine the son was just a tad overwhelmed, because Christmas—and the entire holiday season—is a *big* deal for us. From the time Ellison and I got married, we joined no less than three other families in perpetual celebration from Thanksgiving through New Year's Day. There was Auntie Ethel and her children, her sister Anna and her husband and children, and Anna's sister-in-law Beulah and adult son Leroy, who are also our daughter's godparents. They'd rotate hosting each of the three holiday festivities at each other's homes, and it was always a blur of activity and fun. On the Christmas Ellison's son was with us, we followed our traditional practice: starting Christmas Eve, we all gathered at the appointed house and brought all our gifts. We ate and prepped the food for the next day's feast, played games, and then separated everyone's gifts before midnight. When the clock struck twelve, we opened only the gifts purchased from a name drawing back on Thanksgiving but saved the rest for later that morning. We did all we could the make the son a part of the bigger family. He stayed with us for about a week.

Finally, he came to California a third time several years later after his high school graduation. That visit was the result of discussions between Ellison and me to have all three of the kids together for their graduations, and Ellison made all the arrangements. Though his son was a year older than Neema, they were graduating seniors at the same time, and Imani was graduating from middle school—so we pulled off yet another surprise, this time on her. Imani's graduation was before Neema's, so Ellison picked him up at the airport, then returned home to get me and Neema and take all of us to Imani's graduation while she was still at school getting ready for her ceremony. When we gathered in the outdoor bleachers, Neema held up a big sign announcing that he was there. From the field, Imani saw the sign, he stood up and waved at her, and she just about lost it. Afterward, we had a party for the three of them complete with catering and a big cake with their names on it. The girls were thrilled, Ellison and I were pleased, and the son seemed happy, too. His visit again lasted for about a week.

Those three visits were the only times the girls and I ever saw Ellison's son. When he got married, we weren't invited to the wedding. When he and his wife started a family, we never saw his children. At no time when he visited us was I referred to as, well, anything. He hardly talked to me directly and never called me anything other than Jacki. I tried to be the bigger person and not take out my hurt on him or anyone else in the family, but it was difficult. Basically, it was as if he was with his dad, his sisters, and Jacki. I was just *there*.

As adults, both Neema and Imani wanted to be a part of

their brother's life, too, but they were rejected. They invited him to their weddings and he said he would come, only to back out at the last moment for one reason or another. That crushed them. Years later, he contacted them when he joined the Marines, but it was only to get personal information about them just in case something happened to him while he was deployed. They blew a gasket over that because they had been trying to have a relationship with him, but the first time he reached out to them was because he had to. Once since then, Imani arranged through social media to meet up with him in Atlanta

I tried to be the bigger person and not take out my hurt on him or anyone else in the family, but it was difficult.

after he had moved there with his mother, and he met two of Imani's children when they were little, but I know nothing more of the visit. Neema pretty much wrote him off.

None of this was easy for Ellison, either. He saw all of this, of course, and felt somewhat responsible, but he didn't know what to do about it. Everyone involved was dealing with some sort of hurt. For a long time, the mother didn't allow Ellison to participate in his son's life other than sending the checks and the occasional phone call. I didn't know why for the longest time, and it left Ellison in a quandary where he couldn't really go to bat for us with her and his son or advocate for a better relationship between all of us. It was what it was.

As far as the checks were concerned, they went out to the mother every month until the son went off to college, at which point we sent the checks directly to him until he left school. We sent the payment at the same time we did our household bills. Sometimes Ellison wrote it and other times, I did, until we got to the point where I was always paying the bills and I started both sending and signing the checks. A couple of months into that transition, the mother called Ellison and told him she didn't want me signing her checks.

My response was blunt. "Well, then tell her not to cash them!"

I was mad. We'd been sending her checks, without fail and without a legal requirement, for a decade, and they had always come from our joint checking account anyway. What difference did it make that my signature was on them? Then, several months later, I had a bona fide fit when she served Ellison with child support papers because she wanted more money.

I called her at work, and I was livid. "Listen," I said, bypassing any get-reacquainted small talk. "If you needed more money, even if you just *wanted* more money, you could've talked to us about it. If we couldn't come to an agreement, then by all means go to the courts. But you didn't give us a chance to work something out, and we've been sending this money faithfully and without a court order." I added, "And how many African-American men are Deadbeat Dads and you can't even find them, and you're not dealing with that kind of guy. But you didn't give us a chance. So if you want to go to court, we are under no obligation at this point to give you anything. You don't get anything until the court decides what will happen." I didn't tell Ellison about the call until after I had made it, and his reaction of, "Okay, whatever," evidenced his frustrated resignation at the whole matter.

In the end, she missed eight months of payments before the matter was settled, resulting in us paying her the same amount we always had been.

I paused, was affirmed by Hazel's steady attentiveness, and took a deep breath. What I was about to share next I'd just found out, and I wasn't sure yet what to do with it. It started when Ellison got a call from his son's mother that led to a couple of long conversations. After the second call, Ellison told me that she said his son was apparently close to having an emotional breakdown that could be PTSD. He said it might be related to his deployment in Afghanistan, his current unemployment, troubles he was having in his marriage, or perhaps even issues his son had with him. Ellison then added that his son told him his life would've been better if Ellison had chosen his mother instead of me.

"He wants to be closer to me," Ellison concluded, "and wants to talk more. We've agreed to work on our relationship."

I looked at my husband. *Instead of me?* The words stung, but again I supposed it was understandable. Undoubtedly, his perception was that we were off in California living this seemingly perfect life as an ideal family. Yet I could see the hopefulness in my husband's face. As a father, he surely coveted the possibility of helping his son through whatever it was he was going through.

And maybe, just maybe, there was an opportunity for me, too.

"How about if I try to connect with him also? Maybe this will be a good time for us to try."

I expected Ellison to think that was a great idea—but he was anything but enthusiastic.

He hesitated before responding. "Well, actually, um, he said that sometimes when he was here, when he was younger, that you were mean to him. Abusive."

I was shocked. "What?" The accusation came out of nowhere and I felt ready to blow a fuse right then and there. But I also had to maintain my composure. Why should I explode since I hadn't done anything wrong? Still, my mind reeled. I had no idea how I could've possibly abused the boy, and I wanted—needed—to know.

"Well," I said, "what did I do?"

"I think you should talk to him about that."

Now I *really* wanted to go off. "I haven't talked to him in his entire life! I doubt that he's going to feel like telling me." My heart was pounding. My voice rose an octave. "If he told you, why can't you tell me?"

"It isn't my place to tell you," Ellison said in a maddeningly businesslike tone. "We'll just end up getting in an argument anyway. So if you need to know, you need to ask him yourself."

Ellison's calmness and his refusal to tell me anything incensed me. He was wrong; our discussions about his son did not *usually* end up in an argument. I tried to slow down my breathing as I ruminated. *Here I am again—alone, apart from the two of you, on the outside. You're taking his side, Ellison, whether you believe it or not, and you're not giving me the chance to even defend myself because I don't even get to know what I did.* But Ellison had already shut down and wasn't going to say another word. It was a common denominator when we did argue; I'd come on too strong, and my emotions would cause Ellison to retreat. So we just sat there, silently together in the same room, but not together at all.

Even as I finished telling this to Hazel, I'd become agitated again and had to remind myself to stay cool. The revelation from Ellison and its aftermath was still fresh. Meanwhile, Hazel looked perplexed. Her confusion started when I first mentioned the abuse claim, and now I think she was just as befuddled as to why Ellison wouldn't reveal to me the details of the accusation. Oddly, she then suggested I contact Al-Anon, an organization she hadn't mentioned before, even when my father's alcoholism was first mentioned. Seeing my reaction, Hazel pointed out that

Al-Anon isn't just about alcoholism but can offer support for anyone who has been emotionally abused. She must've believed that's what was going on with me and Ellison.

I courteously accepted the information as she printed it out, and we concluded the session with Hazel saying we'd go into the memories next week. But as I got up to leave, I'd already made up my mind. There was no way I was going to contact Al-Anon about this.

Over the next couple of days, I remained irritated with Ellison for not sharing what his son said about me. I ended up asking Ellison for his son's address, but even then, he put up resistance, saying he'd only give me his phone number so I could ask for the address myself. That wasn't going to do me any good. I'd already told Ellison that I didn't feel speaking to the son was best. Frustrated, I turned to Facebook, went to his son's page, asked him for an address, and he responded with it a few minutes later. Address in hand, I decided to write a letter to Ellison's son—a personal,

Even as I finished telling this to Hazel, I'd become agitated again and had to remind myself to stay cool.

handwritten communication versus an email or a post. Although I already had plenty of stationery options at home, I went out and bought a special card just for him. It was white with a classy white foil trim on the front. I wrote:

> *Your Dad tells me that the two of you have been talking and making an effort to build more of a relationship with each other. I'm happy for you that you're working towards getting closer to your Dad. It's something he's always wanted.*

I am writing to let you know that I would be more than willing to establish a relationship with you also. Although I hope over time we can be in touch more, I fully support whatever your choice is. The door is open at any time to talk. In any case, please know that I wish only the best for you and your family.

Jacki

I didn't mention his accusation or how much it wounded me. Nor did I tell Ellison that I sent it. I put the date on it—September 21, 2016—and put it in the mail.

The rest of the week, I wondered how Hazel was going to react to my decision to send the letter, and what was going to happen when we finally delved into my memories of Ellison and all that time he spent with his son—and away from me.

Chapter 6

At the start of our session, I told Hazel about the letter and why I felt I needed to write it and she was nothing but supportive. She said what I did was healthy and that the ball was now in his court and that there was nothing more I could do.

I was relieved. "I'm glad I did it. I feel a sense of closure," I told her. "Either he'll respond, or he won't, but I can't carry this baggage around with me anymore." Then I thought, as if speaking to the son in my mind, *And, if you don't respond, it'll be on you, and quite frankly, it's your loss.*

With that, the EMDR machine was switched on and we went into the first memory. I was twenty-one years old, in my apartment, and sitting on my olive green, orange, and mustard yellow plaid couch. The matching orange lamp the only light on in the room. I was staring out my window looking at everything outside—and at nothing at all. It seemed as if I had been sucked into a black hole with no hope of escaping from its persistent inward pull. It was the weekend and Ellison was with his son, just as he said he would be. By then, all my friends from high school and afterward had moved on. There was no one to call, no one to hang out with to pass the time.

I couldn't think of anything to do. I didn't want to be one of those chicks who just sat around waiting for her guy to call, but that's exactly what I was. It was just me and my utter aloneness—for the next hour, the rest of the night, and the remainder of the weekend. The only time I was with others was at church, but Ellison wasn't there, either, because he was away.

With his son. Not with me.

The memory was less about what I did and more about my lingering, pervasive, depressive sadness. My eyes were closed, and I felt the buzzing of the EMDR paddles, but it was as if I had traveled back in time, back into the void of my loneliness. I sank into it, wallowed in it, experienced it anew. It was just like my funks, only worse.

I don't recall how many times we stopped and then went back into the memory, but we didn't complete the process that day. I don't recall much about how I felt in-between the memory trips, except that all my exhausting emotions were felt inwardly. At the close of the session, I had to put the memory away and go to my safe place—and then I successfully didn't think about it again for the next week. For the first time, I realized how truly grateful I was for my safe place, and because the previous EMDR treatments had worked so well, I remained confident I'd get through this memory and the ones still to come. It was hard, so hard—but I was glad I was getting to them.

By the time I returned to Hazel's office, I still hadn't heard a reply from Ellison's son. I put that out of my mind, though, as we continued working on my lonely apartment memory. We went back and forth a few more times, and with each trip I became aware of how pathetic I'd been to just sit there on my couch, mope, and wait for a call or visit that I knew wasn't coming. While that made me feel sad, it also propelled me forward to realize that my perception of my value wasn't about Ellison. It was all about me. Whether he chose to spend time with his son, or anybody else, over me did not, therefore, make me unimportant. It took a session-and-a-half, but I got there: my negative belief of "I am not important to Ellison" was replaced with the positive perception, "I am important."

I was encouraged, but I knew I had more to cover—much more. I set down the EMDR machine paddles, took a breath, and proceeded to tell Hazel about something that, until recently, I hadn't shared with anyone else.

From the start of our marriage, Ellison and I argued. These disagreements followed a pattern similar to the one I'd introduced to Hazel the week before when detailing how he and I interacted after he revealed his son's claim of abuse. I'd get emotional and loud, he'd either give me a response I didn't like or none at all, I'd get louder and more emotional, and then he'd shut down entirely. We did this a lot about topics great and small, and we'd rarely resolved anything. I guess we just didn't know any better, and it certainly didn't do our young marriage any favors, because there were two times when our lack of communication was so frustrating that he apparently came to a conclusion that he'd had enough.

The first time came right after we had moved from New York to California. We were still newlyweds and Neema was almost a year old. It had been a normal day at work, and I arrived downstairs to the apartment just below ours to pick up Neema from our babysitter. I chatted with her a bit, then gathered the baby in my arms and headed upstairs. I unlocked the front door, stepped inside, and set Neema down to toddle about so I could pass through the living room and by the kitchen and dining rooms areas into the bedroom. I tossed my purse on the bed, looked about—and immediately knew something was terribly wrong.

Things were missing. Not all things. Just those that belonged to my husband.

I went into the bathroom. His toiletries were gone. I opened the closet. His clothes were gone.

Anything that belonged to Ellison, anything at all, was gone.

My stomach sank, and my temple throbbed to the hammering beat of my pulse. I returned to the kitchen and dialed the phone on the wall. Ring. Another ring. I was certain he wasn't going to answer when he picked up.

"This is Ellison." The greeting was formal since he was at his desk at work.

"This is Jacki. I just got home. What's going on?"

Our back and forth exchange about whose fault it was didn't last long, probably less than a minute. It ended with him saying, "I'm just gone. I can't do this anymore."

I hung up the phone as gently as I could, trying to steady my nerves. I was terrified. *We just moved here, all the way across*

My stomach sank, and my temple throbbed to the hammering beat of my pulse.

the country. Not only do I not know this place, I don't know anyone here other than the co-workers I just met. All of my support is back home. We just bought a new car. The rent here is double what I was paying in White Plains. I looked down at Neema, playing on the floor without a care. *I have a baby.*

What am I going to do?

Ellison and I had started attending a small church in San Jose called Eastside Church of God in Christ. I went to the pastor, told him what had happened, and he said he thought he knew someone in the congregation who could help me out and maybe even rent out a room to me and my daughter.

That was my introduction to Ethel—who'd quickly become Auntie Ethel—and she took us in. Ethel had two sons, ages fifteen and twelve, and a five-year-old daughter. She was an insurance claims adjuster and a widow; her husband had died from lung cancer within the last year. Ethel was mild-mannered, had a soft spirit, and cooked for all of us and watched Neema when I went to choir rehearsal. I paid her a small rent, and because she made us feel so much like family, I helped with household chores, cleaning the kitchen and folding clothes, though it wasn't expected of me. Even more, when I had questions about Neema, Ethel provided ready answers, and it wasn't unusual for the two of us to hang out together in her bedroom at night and chit-chat. I confided in her, and she became like a big sister or second mom. She even taught me how to cook. She was such a blessing in my life—and still is.

We remained with Auntie Ethel for the next year while Ellison and I talked occasionally at work or when we'd see each other when he visited Neema. He didn't attend church while we were apart. After a while, he started expressing that he wanted to get back together and reunite his family. Ethel was very supportive of us, knowing that I still loved him and wanted to stay married. When we finally reconciled, there was no big hoopla. Ellison returned, we found a townhouse, moved into it, and he came back to church.

I then told Hazel that our tendency to argue, and the methodology we followed, went unaddressed and only worsened—until a few years later, shortly after Imani was born. I came home from work again, this time to find a letter on the nightstand—not to me, but to the landlord. It was from Ellison. It stated that he was moving out. I took a quick look around to see that all his stuff was still there, so he hadn't left yet. But the fact that he formally copied me on the letter implied that since both of our names were on the lease, the rent on the townhouse was now my responsibility, along with all the other bills.

No discussion. No warning. He was just gone. Again.

By then Imani had been born, so I proceeded to find a place for the three of us since there was no way I could afford the townhouse. Ironically, I found an apartment in the same complex where we used to live, and Ellison ended up staying in the townhouse for a while before finding another place. For the longest time, I simply did what I had to do. I took the girls to the babysitter, went to work, picked them up, fixed us dinner, and got them ready for bed—and then I'd crash in a stupor before repeating it all over again the next morning. That was all the energy I had. I gained solace and strength from church where, again, Ellison was not in attendance. But I felt like I was constantly on the verge of a nervous breakdown.

Finally, I decided I couldn't go on like that. Since moving to California, I had talked to Mommy almost every day on the phone, and we also wrote letters back and forth. She was in Florida by then, and our relationship was fine—the difficulties of my adolescent years pushed aside by distance, time, and the fact that we were both older and a tad wiser. I shared with her about how I was feeling, and I knew she could tell just from the sound of my voice that I was doing worse than I let on.

After volunteering to take the girls for a while, an offer I appreciated but declined because I felt they were all I had at that moment to keep me from completely falling apart, Mommy said, "Jacki, you were raised in church." Her tone was encouraging but firm. "You know the Lord. You know your answers are always with Him. You need to get back to what you know."

As I considered her words, I realized that although I indeed had been going to church, I had never really talked to God about anything of consequence, much less about my broken marriage. After I got off the phone, I checked on the girls to make sure they were sound asleep, then went into the living room and collapsed onto the couch. Strengthened and reassured by Mommy's care and her exhortation, I gathered my resolve, and then sat up, bent over, and closed my eyes.

"God," I pled quietly, "I need your help. I am okay with whatever your will is going to be. If it's your will for us to get back together, then I'm okay with that; if not, I'm okay with that, too." Through that basic, heartfelt prayer, I came to terms with my situation, let it go—and for the first time, really, in my entire life, I learned to trust God. I'd always been able to make my way through whatever came my way, but this time I knew no one except Him could fix this.

From then on, I joined the church choir and became more active in Sunday school and the women's ministry. It was the first time I really dove into church work, and it set the standard for involved service that I'd follow at church for years to come. I saw Ellison whenever he'd come to see the girls, and sometimes when I had company from church over to the apartment for dinner. But I was no longer pining after him. In fact, I was working, paying the bills, and getting along fine without Ellison—so much so that when he decided he was ready to come back, my pastor had to convince me to do it, arguing that I surely didn't want to spend the rest of my life alone. I also decided I didn't want the girls growing up without their father being there.

For the first time, really, in my entire life, I learned to trust God.

This time around, we also made more of a commitment to

our marriage—enough, anyway, to warrant a remarriage ceremony. It was at Auntie Ethel's house (she did all of the cooking
while I ordered the cake and the flowers) and was attended by
about thirty people, mostly folks from Eastside. Even during our
planning of the event, though, Ellison and I had some disagreements, and we still didn't deal with our argumentative ways. We
renewed our vows, hoping that alone was somehow going to
take care of the problem.

Hazel listened, took copious notes, and we concluded our session for that day without doing any EMDR. That turned out to be
a good thing because, by the time I arrived the following week, I
had a third story of strife between me and Ellison to share with
her—one that was much more recent. I took my seat across
from her desk and stifled my embarrassment. Though Hazel was
easy to talk to, I wasn't eager to share yet another tale of marital
woe. But I knew I had to. *Here we go again*, I thought, before
plunging in.

In 2015, even while I was working on *Cancer With Grace*,
Ellison and I were in the midst of one of the worst periods of our
relationship. Money was always an issue with us. Most recently,
he didn't feel we had enough and that I should be working to
help make up the difference. Because of this and any other number of smaller issues blown out of proportion, he and I argued
constantly, and I was fed up. I felt that whatever I shared with
Ellison was twisted around to where it ended up being my fault.
It seemed that whatever I said to him was wrong, whatever I did
was wrong, and if I didn't say or do anything, that was wrong, too.
He often told me that he likewise believed whatever he said or
did wasn't enough for me. I'd pretty much lost hope one morning

when I arrived at the church office for my administrator duties. I grabbed my notepad and went in to see Pastor Michael for our usual start-of-the-day meeting to get my assignments from him—and without a word, I practically fell into the couch in front of his desk. I was in tears and I didn't mince any words.

"I feel like I want to get a divorce," I stammered through the sobs.

Pastor Michael gasped, and his mouth fell open. He asked me to tell him what was going on, and I did. That settled me down and helped me get my bearings. He then asked if I'd be open to marriage counseling with him for me and Ellison, and I said yes.

No sooner had I responded that Pastor Michael's phone chimed. "It's from Ellison," he said. "It says, 'I think Jacki and I need counseling. If she's open to it, would you do it?'"

He looked at me for a response. At first, I was thoroughly unimpressed. "Sure. Of course, he does," I said, then sighed and conceded, "but yes, I'll do it."

That evening when Ellison got home from work, I told him about my breakdown with Pastor Michael and my decision regarding his text. Then, thinking it would be a helpful and honest way to initiate our soon-to-start counseling, I told him, "I just want you to know—I told Pastor Michael I felt like I wanted a divorce."

And, as had been the case recently, whatever I said, regardless of my motivation, was once more apparently wrong.

"You said you want a divorce?"

That was all he said, but I could tell that it was best not to pursue it any further. I stayed quiet, and Ellison retreated into his office.

The next morning, I went into the office because I needed to reset the modem located on his desk. As I rebooted the device, I saw two things on top of some other papers, sitting in plain sight: a pamphlet showing apartment vacancies and legal separation papers.

I was befuddled. *Why are these things here?* What I had said to Ellison the night before didn't even occur to me. Why would it? When I said it, I knew the context; I didn't really *want* a divorce. Besides, we were about to start counseling to work on the marriage. It made no sense.

I decided to keep my discovery to myself, though, as the counseling began. I wanted to see if Ellison was going to bring it up first, but after the first two sessions with Pastors Michael and Maria, he hadn't. By the third session, I didn't think the rough, sometimes abrasive "he said, she said" debates were going any-where or accomplishing anything, despite how many times both pastors said Ellison and I needed to be "all in" with the process. Things escalated until I said in near-hopeless frustration, "I don't think Ellison is 'all in' on this at all—especially since I found separation papers and an apartment pamphlet on his desk." I then added, "And I don't *want* a divorce. That's *why* I agreed to counseling."

Pastor Michael was about to speak when he was cut off by my husband. "Doesn't matter," Ellison said, matter-of-fact. "You said it. That's what you want. I'm going to give it to you."

I sassed back, "No. That's *not* what I want."

For the next several days after that session, Ellison came home from work, said a quick "hello," then went straight to his office. No hug. No kiss. No nothing. One of the worst things you can do to another human being is ignore them—and that's exactly what Ellison was doing to me. So each night I sat, watched TV until I was ready for bed, and allowed the desperate anguish to build up inside of me until it just had to burst.

I went into the bedroom, and by the time I got under the covers, I was weeping uncontrollably. Ellison was laying on his side, his back to me. I started begging.

"Don't leave. *Please don't leave!*"

He didn't turn over. He didn't try to touch or comfort me as he had so often done in years past, especially when I had cancer. Instead, as though he was noting the next day's weather forecast, he said, "I don't think I can stay."

I cried myself to sleep. I thought it was over. We were supposed to return to counseling a few days later, but after that, I decided I just wasn't going to go. What was the point? It wasn't working. I called Pastor Michael to inform him of my decision. He tried to talk me out of it, but I was so steeped in angry resignation that I rudely blew him off.

Unbeknownst to me, Ellison got together with Pastors Michael and Maria, because the next Tuesday night, when he was already away at the church for a regularly scheduled meeting with the pastors as a member of the church's leadership team, I received a text message from Pastor Michael. It read, "I want you to come down to the church."

The church was on the other side of town and it was already getting late. I punched in my reply. "I'm not coming."

The phone chimed seconds later. "If you don't come down to the church tonight, we're going to show up to your house on Thursday."

That surprised—and irritated—me. I didn't want him and his wife to just appear at the front door so I could refuse to let them in. I wanted to throw the phone across the room. "Fine," I typed. "I'll be there soon."

I hardly remember the long drive and my car was probably running on the fumes generated by my anger, because by the time I arrived, I had my attitude *full* on. I felt like I was being ambushed—especially after, not finding the pastors at their home on the church property as expected, I walked into the sanctuary to see them and Ellison waiting for me. *What's this?* I thought. *How long have the three of them been here talking?*

Pastor Maria began. "Miss Jacki, let me tell you what happened to me." She proceeded to tell me a story of when her and

Pastor Michael were having a big misunderstanding with their daughter, and how Pastor Maria felt ganged up on by both of them. I could tell what she was doing. She was trying to get me to relate how I felt about her situation. But the more she talked, the angrier I got. *This has nothing to do with what I'm feeling or going through*, I thought. *Again, nobody has heard my side of the story, so you don't know the full story.* Then Pastors Michael and

This has nothing to do with what I'm feeling or going through, I thought.

Maria both started talking about how they had dealt with their own marriage issues in the past, describing what they had done and trying to get Ellison and me to do the same exercises. But I was resolute. *This is just a waste of time. I don't think it's going to work. It hasn't worked until now.*

I was numb and done.

The whole thing, this intervention of sorts, lasted for a couple of hours. We ended in prayer, and right before it was time to leave, Pastor Michael was insistent. "Jacki, you need to never mention divorce again, and Ellison, you must stop passively threatening to leave your wife."

We drove home, of course, in separate cars, but I think if we had been in the same vehicle, we wouldn't have talked about what had just happened. When we got home, Ellison went directly into his office and returned about twenty minutes later with the pamphlet, the legal separation papers, and a pen. He then started walking toward the door to our garage and motioned for me to join him. "Would you come with me?" he asked.

Not sure why we were going into the garage, I followed him. He gave me the pen and had me write the word "divorce" on the back of the separation papers. Then he said, "We are going to put these papers and the pamphlet, and everything that they represent, in the shredder, and we are not going to talk about it, or deal with it, ever again. This is it."

At first, I thought the gesture was kinda dumb, but as the grinding sound of the shredder sliced apart what had almost done the same thing to our marriage, I decided to give him—and us—the benefit of the doubt. *It may be just a gesture*, I thought, *but up until now, there was been nothing. We still have a lot of work to do, but let's see where this goes.*

Ellison returned to his office and I settled myself in front of the television, and we retained our usual evening routine until we went to bed. But there was a difference. The overall atmosphere between us was lighter—and that was the first time I really felt we were both on the same page and not holding anything against one another.

Our counseling with Pastors Michael and Maria ended in September 2015, and our relationship continued to heal and improve over the next six months leading up to the Sunday morning funk in February 2016 that brought about my PTSD diagnosis. Now here I was, eight months later with Hazel in October, and I took a deep breath. Now that I felt I'd revealed all that I had to share about the on-again, off-again events that nearly destroyed my marriage, I was relieved and no longer embarrassed. *That wasn't as hard as I thought it would be.*

Hazel then decided it was time to once again do EMDR. I took the paddles in my hands, closed my eyes, and thought back over all three incidents, and really, about our entire marriage. As I reflected on the events from the year before, I dealt with anxiety about abandonment. As opposed to the other times when Ellison left me, I had no job, no other source of income, and certainly didn't want to burden myself off on one of the girls had we actually divorced, and I ended up being homeless.

But once again the EMDR did its good work—and by the time I was through with that same session, I had replaced my negative beliefs of either, "I'm not good enough," or "I am not important to Ellison," with "I am good enough" and "I am important."

Now that I was getting stable through therapy and Ellison and I were doing better in our marriage, we decided it was important to meet with Pastors Michael and Maria to let them know what was going on with me. It had been a year since the "intervention" at the church, and the anger of the night had long been forgotten. They were doing whatever they could then to help us, and I'd come to appreciate how their determination pushed back against my stubbornness. When we had little to no hope, they still had hope for us—and we'd made it through. Still, I was scared to reveal my mental issues to them because the only other church person I'd ever done that with was my pastor in Phoenix, and that turned out horribly. But I had also missed about a month of church back when I went off my medications, and I did want to give Pastors Michael and Maria an explanation for my absence.

We arranged to have dinner with them at a restaurant and kept it to chit-chat through the meal. When we ordered dessert, though, I knew the time had come. The relationship between

Ellison and me had improved so much by then—we had both let go of the past, and as a result were now less prone to react in a way that would start an argument, and more often thinking things through first and then proactively discussing issues with one another instead of reacting out of frustration or misunderstanding—that he had once more become a stabilizer and source of security to me. I inched closer to Ellison, then placed my hand on his knee, and finally wrapped my arm around his; I needed his strength to make it through my big revelation. I had no idea what Pastors Michael and Maria were going to say or how they were going to take the news. I was terrified they wouldn't understand.

I opened my mouth, and between comforting bits of creamy cheesecake, I got it all out, from the first breakdown all the way through the news that I had been seeing a therapist and an overview of how our sessions had gone. I revealed everything except the suicide attempts. Pastors Michael and Maria were quiet, listened attentively—and to my utter relief, were totally understanding.

"Whatever you need," Pastor Michael said, "just let us know. We're glad you shared this with us. It won't go any further than this table." Pastor Maria added, "If you get to church and feel like you don't want to put on that 'Miss Jacki' hat, you don't have to. We've got you."

They cared about Jacki the person. Me. That was all. And it was plenty.

Though they said they had never dealt with anyone in their church, much less on staff, who had depression, anxiety, or PTSD, they weren't judgmental in any way. The evening ended in hugs, and with each one I breathed a massive sigh of relief. It was clear: they weren't concerned about Jacki the church member or Jacki the office administrator; they cared about Jacki the person. Me. That was all. And it was plenty.

As it turned out, I only returned to Hazel once more, in early November. She asked how I was, and I told her I was doing well. We discussed all the target memories once more and how I felt about all of them—and by the close of the session, we both agreed that my therapy was complete.

Hazel said she was proud of me. I appreciated that.

Even more, I was proud of myself. That was priceless.

And it was about to set up the next unexpected challenge in my life. But it wasn't one that was going to hinder my growing sense of healing and wholeness. Instead, it was going to help it— and position me to reach out to others, especially those who are churchgoers, dealing with the harsh realities and stigmas that come with mental illness.

Part Two

The Diva Reveals

Chapter 7

Ava Rose and I talk to one another every single day. It's been that way since we started our friendship at the church in Phoenix—the same church I was ultimately left—and continues even though Ava Rose's job as a school teacher forces our weekday calls to take place pretty early in the morning. We are girlfriends and confidants despite the nearly thirty years of age difference between us.

It was in one of those conversations in late 2016 that Ava Rose told me about someone who revealed to her a horrific trauma she experienced when she was a little girl. Now a young adult, the person told Ava Rose that she knew her memories of that unspeakable event were a problem that had negatively impacted everything from how she saw herself and her place in life to how she raised her children and the failure of her marriage.

When Ava Rose suggested she consider therapy, the person responded in a way I was starting to realize was far too common, especially among Christians.

"I gave it some thought," she said, "but I just thought God would fix it. Besides, the idea of going to therapy makes me nervous and uncomfortable."

It made me think, *What would that person say if she knew I dealt with depression?* Then, I also pondered, *I wonder if she'd get therapy for herself if she knew I had PTSD and had gone through therapy?*

Then, as Ava Rose began to wrap up our time together, her dialogue was briefly overridden by another voice, one that I'd heard several years before in the same way—concise, unmistakable, and filled with purpose and love.

"Jacki," the Lord said, His tone soothingly familiar to my spirit, "write a book about it."

This isn't about me, I remembered. *It's about how my testimony will give Him glory.*

Within the week, I was back in my editor's office, and we started work on the book you are now reading.

Right down the road from my home is the office for the National Alliance of Mental Illness of Southern Arizona. It reports that mental illness affects one out of every five people in the United States. That's a staggering number, made even more relevant if you envision it in the context of your local church. Picture in your mind your Sunday morning congregation, and then think: one out of every five people you see in your mind's eye are either dealing with mental illness themselves or has a family member or loved one who is.

But here's the problem. Have you ever heard the topic of mental illness addressed from the pulpit of your church? The Sunday school classroom? The small group Bible study session? Likely not—and that's a shame when you consider how many people in each of those settings are dealing with the reality of mental illness.

Why is there no mention of mental illness in churches? It's ignored—and when we as Christians don't address something, we don't understand it, and that lack of understanding breeds silence. We just don't talk about it.

I remember back when I was a youngster in church and how Christians then didn't talk about sex. There could be a lady in the church with a big belly, but when she came back a few years later with a small child in tow, nobody talked about it. My mother never, ever talked to me about sex. It was taboo, though it was understood that you certainly didn't have sex outside of marriage.

Today, sex is not nearly as ignored in churches as it used to be—but mental illness is. It's today's taboo in Christian church culture. Yet essential to destigmatizing anything is to talk about it. Even more, it should be talked about by leadership within the church, from the pulpit to the classroom. When Christians start treating mental illness as something we don't need to hide in our congregations, our churches will become a safe place where dialogue is open, vulnerability is encouraged, and despairing hearts can receive comfort and hope.

Not once have I ever heard a message preached about the physical or mental well-being of a person.

Recognizing the silence

Dr. Martin Luther King, Jr. once said, "Our lives begin to end the day we become silent about things that matter." I've been a churchgoer all my life. Specifically, I have attended African American Pentecostal churches, and not once have I ever heard a message preached about the physical or mental well-being of a person. This is because Christian churches, by and large, focus on the care of the soul—the part of a human being's triune makeup (body, soul, and spirit) that determines if our spirit will spend eternity in Heaven or in Hell. This emphasis on soul care asserts that all our efforts here on Earth are to be done with the final destination in mind. If we avoid sinful behavior, and seek forgiveness when we do sin, then our soul will be well and our spirit ready for Heaven when we die. If we sin and do not seek forgiveness, our soul will not be well, placing our spirit in eternal jeopardy.

Regardless of where you stand on the subject of "once saved, always saved" salvation, this prioritization of soul and spirit in Christian churches has resulted in a deemphasis or all-around negligence of the health of our body and mind, especially our emotional and psychological selves.

Yet when you look at Scripture, there is a myriad of teaching on the mind that affects how we as Christians should view mental illness and those among us who are impacted by it. Here are just a few, only from the New Testament, of the 160-plus uses of the word "mind" in the Bible:

- "All the believers were one in heart and mind. No one claimed that any of their possessions was their own, but they shared everything they had." (Acts 4:32)
- "I see another law at work in me, waging war against the law of my mind and making me a prisoner of the law of sin at work within me. What a wretched man I am! Who will rescue me from this body that is subject to death? Thanks be to God, who delivers me through Jesus Christ our Lord! So then, I myself in my mind am a slave to God's law, but in my sinful nature a slave to the law of sin." (Romans 7:23-25)
- "The mind governed by the flesh is death, but the mind governed by the Spirit is life and peace." (Romans 8:6)

- "Do not conform to the pattern of this world, but be transformed by the renewing of your mind. Then you will be able to test and approve what God's will is— his good, pleasing and perfect will." (Romans 12:2)
- "May the God who gives endurance and encouragement give you the same attitude of mind toward each other that Christ Jesus had, so that with one mind and one voice you may glorify the God and Father of our Lord Jesus Christ." (Romans 15:5-6)
- "For, 'Who has known the mind of the Lord so as to instruct him?' But we have the mind of Christ." (1 Corinthians 2:16)
- "You were taught, with regard to your former way of life, to put off your old self, which is being corrupted by its deceitful desires; to be made new in the attitude of your minds; and to put on the new self, created to be like God in true righteousness and holiness." (Ephesians 4:22-23)
- "In your relationships with one another, have the same mindset as Christ Jesus." (Philippians 2:5)
- "Set your minds on things above, not on earthly things." (Colossians 3:2)

I am not a theologian; I am a layperson student of the Word of God. But it seems clear just from this small sample that an *understanding of the mind*—how it contributes to our unity as believers in Christ and our ability to honor Him, how our thinking impacts our obedience to and intimacy with God, and how our thoughts can affect our knowledge of His purposes for our lives—is important to the Lord and therefore vital to how we live as a Christian. Yet when I've heard these passages included in church preaching or teaching, their full context regarding a person's mental health is rarely brought out.

Take, for example, Paul's revelation that we as Christians have "the mind of Christ." It isn't solely from a spiritual perspective that this statement is true. Yes, through our salvation, we are given His mind; it's a wonderful, miraculous spiritual reality. But it's also true that we have access to Christ's thought processes—to how He confronts a problem, how He thinks it through and analyzes it, and how He comes to a decision about it. Even more, this entry into Christ's mind also allows us to discover how He dealt with the pressures He felt, the anxieties He experienced, and even the mental anguish He endured.

When Jesus learned that His dear friend Lazarus had died, He went to Lazarus' sisters Martha and Mary to comfort them. Faced with their grief and the mourning of others, we are told that He wept (John 11:35), manifesting His pain and identifying with the grief of those around Him. When Jesus went into Gethsemane to pray just before the events that led to His crucifixion, He felt so "sorrowful and troubled" (Matthew 26:37) that His sweat "was like drops of blood." (Luke 22:44) When Jesus was on the cross and experienced separation from His Father, the one on whom He had relied to keep Him mentally and spiritually centered throughout His time on Earth, it tore Him up so badly that He cried out in agony (Mark 15:34).

These demonstrations of the Son of God's humanness make Him utterly relatable to those who have mental illness and to their families. They show that He continued onward and fulfilled the purposes His Father had for Him, even while experiencing untold stress and unease. Jesus faced mental trauma and dealt with it—and now Christians have that same mind *within* them. Yet we rarely hear of this humanness in our churches, and when we do, it is never addressed in the context of what it teaches to those who are mentally ill or dealing with mental illness within our congregations. Instead, mental illness is often intertwined with weakness or a lack of faith. Christians dealing with depression, PTSD, or other mental ailments are not encouraged to seek counseling or medication but are exhorted to just pray harder and have more faith. If they'd just do that, they're told, all their problems will go away.

For a long time, I didn't know that I was dealing with mental illness, and I remember now, looking back at those times, how people at church simply assumed that I had a bad attitude or was in a bad mood. "She's just difficult," they'd say, or, "She's obviously not getting her way," when all that time I was likely dealing with depression. People just wrote it off. Not once did anyone give me the benefit of the doubt that something else might be going on. Today, they'd likely respond like Ellison did to my doctor's PTSD diagnosis: "Now it makes sense." But back then it was never even considered. I was told to go pray about it— or they'd say, "I'm going to pray for you about your attitude." I never considered that I needed professional help because no one in the church ever considered it. Besides, I didn't feel I could argue against their advice or counter, "You know what? I don't want to just pray about it," even though that was how I often felt. Likewise, I never knew anyone from church who went to a doctor for anything else but a medical issue. I never even heard of anyone going to the pastor to get counseling.

If you come to church and call yourself a Christian, you should be okay.

It just wasn't talked about. None of it. The assumption was—and, in most cases, still is—that if you come to church and call yourself a Christian, you should be okay. You shouldn't have any problems because "you've got Jesus." And you certainly shouldn't have a mental illness.

Possession clarification

During my therapy, I mentioned to Hazel that my aunt had schizophrenia. My brother David also has the disease. In my aunt's case, no one in the family ever mentioned her condition by name. I understood that she was "different"—she talked to herself, and she was sometimes heard speaking aloud in varying voices—but I was told, "That's just the way she is." Every now and then, she'd sign herself into a hospital until she "felt better," but it wasn't until later as an adult that I learned that hospital was a psychiatric one.

As a child, David acted out, was mean, got into fights, and was the one who wandered off from the rest of us. He often got lost and was always perceived as the "odd guy out" among my siblings. When he was diagnosed with schizophrenia as a young adult, he was prescribed medication but sometimes didn't take it, resulting in him having episodes. At Mommy's funeral, for example, we were lining up as a family to proceed into the church sanctuary when I looked back to notice David out of line and out the door, taking pictures of birds on his cell phone. Considering the moment, I was annoyed, until I remembered his condition and the moments of flightiness it can cause. Later, all of us gathered at a restaurant for dinner. It was loud and crowded, and just after we took our seats, David looked at us.

"I can't stay in here," he muttered. "I'm hearing voices."

Then I remembered, *That's right. He even watches TV with the audio muted because he hears other voices coming out of the TV. With all the people talking in here, it must be really hard for him.* I glanced at him, then at my sister. She knew he had schizophrenia; we all did. But of everyone there, she was clearly the most frightened and agitated, not knowing what was going to happen next.

"Are you going to be okay to stay and eat?" I asked him. "We won't be here long."

He said he was—and he made it through the meal. But it was sad. Over the years, no one else in the family had ever taken the time to try to figure out what was going on with him. Hearing voices is part of his disease, and in large groups of people the condition will usually worsen.

Perhaps because of the silence about mental illness that pervades the Christian church, no one has ever suggested that my aunt or brother were demon possessed—yet it's likely they assumed as much. In fact, many psychologists insist all accounts of demon possession, including those cited in the Bible, are a primitive way to describe mental illness. I couldn't disagree more. Take this scene from Mark 1:21-26:

"They went to Capernaum, and when the Sabbath came, Jesus went into the synagogue and began to teach. The people were amazed at his teaching, because he taught them as one who had authority, not as the teachers of the law. Just then a man in their synagogue who was possessed by an impure spirit cried out, 'What do you want with us, Jesus of Nazareth? Have you come to destroy us? I know who you are—the Holy One of God!' 'Be quiet!' said Jesus sternly. 'Come out of him!' The impure spirit shook the man violently and came out of him with a shriek."

The context is clear. An outside, evil force controlled this man, and Jesus expelled the spirit with His word alone. No contrived exorcism ritual was required. This pattern repeats itself in all the other demon possession accounts in the Bible, and it is never said or implied that these were manifestations of mental illness.

I am mentally ill. I am not demon possessed. It's vital for all believers, especially pastors and other church leaders, to make this delineation because Scripture makes this delineation. Yet it's somehow easier for some Christians to believe another believer is oppressed, or even possessed, by an evil spirit than to accept they have a mental illness. They can't fathom the idea that a born-again, Spirit-filled, washed-in-the-blood-of-the-Lamb believer can have a mental illness.

There must be another reason

This perception has forced some Christians to find other explanations why believers with mental illness are "afflicted" the way they are or behave the way they do. Christians who are mentally

Christians who are mentally ill are sometimes told they are being tested, or even punished, by God.

ill are sometimes told they are being tested, or even punished, by God, "put through the fire" so that they can learn some vital spiritual lesson. Remember the story in the book of Job? Most of the account is a discourse between Job, a man of God who was experiencing great mental and physical anguish, and his three "friends," Eliphaz, Bildad, and Zophar. They had "heard about all the troubles that had come upon him" and "set out from their homes and met together by agreement to go and sympathize with him and comfort him." (Job 2:11)

But they neither pitied nor consoled Job. Time and again,

they accused him of sinning against God. "Surely, you've done something wrong," they pleaded. "Just confess your wrongdoing, and this punishment will cease." Though he despaired severely, Job defended himself to them and declared his trust in the Lord before them. At the end of the book, we discover that God never abandoned Job, but was always there in his suffering. He delivered Job and helped him see His purposes in his affliction.

The story never suggests Job was mentally ill, but the reaction of his so-called friends is indicative of how Christians respond to their fellow believers who have a mental illness. Yet being mentally ill is no more a test or punishment from God as is having a physical illness such as diabetes or cancer. In *Cancer With Grace*, I contended that God never gave me cancer—but used my cancer experience to help me draw closer to Him and to show His love and grace to others. In the same way, God can and often will use our mental illnesses to cause us to trust Him more and even honor Him before other people. But mental illness is never punitive from God or intentionally given to us by the Lord.

This shift away from stigmatizing mental illness as a moral failing or the result of personal sin and moving toward a more thorough preaching and teaching about what the Bible says about our minds and mental well-being will position Christian churches to offset the silence—and offer more than soul care to begin to support and sustain those with mental health issues and their families.

This is essential, because mentally ill people are coming into our churches every Sunday, and they are feeling anything but comfortable and welcome.

Chapter 8

Walk into any African American church on a given Sunday—and you'll have a memorable experience. An usher, clad in an all-white, knee-length, nurse-type uniform dress to distinguish her from other members of the congregation, will greet you at the door with a handshake or a hug. Seated in the pews, you'll see gentlemen dressed in suits, with matching ties and pocket squares, their feet shod in polished Stacy Adams shoes complimented by snazzy socks. The women will be in designer outfits sparkling with glitter and rhinestones, their nails immaculately manicured and hair coiffed to perfection. Some of the ladies will be wearing hats, the more flamboyant the better. (Mommy always wore one peppered with rhinestones, adorned with a face net, and topped with a bouquet of flowers or some sort of bird feather poking out of it.) The children will be utterly adorable, mini replicas of their parents.

It's a warm, colorful scene. But now imagine a young woman with mental illness—I'll call her Loretta—entering that lively setting. All morning, she staved off her emotions, telling herself to just make it to the house of the Lord. She could barely summon the strength to get out of bed, much less dress to the nines to go to church. She managed to slip on a pair of jeans, a t-shirt, and sandals, only to find herself suppressing panic as she pulled into the parking lot.

Heart pounding, Loretta takes deep breaths to try to settle herself down. *You can do this,* she exhorts within. *Church will be good for you. It'll calm you down. The Lord loves you.* Determined, she shakily walks up to the entrance, sees the usher, and bravely puts on her best smiley face to accept the usher's greeting, resisting an irrational urge caused by her nervousness to recoil from her touch.

As Loretta steps from the foyer into the sanctuary, the service starts. She hears the minister call the gathering to order with a hearty "Praise the Lord!" Everyone repeats the words in unison, then the minister bellows, "I said Praise the Lord, saints!" They echo him, even louder. Then it happens once more, louder yet and punctuated by thumping chords on the organ. She scoots into a back-corner pew and slams her eyelids shut against the cacophony of sound, willing her once-more increased pulse to slow down.

I like what I'm hearing. I really do. But it's so noisy. So joyful. So—overwhelming. Slowly opening her eyes, she looks at the couple next to her. They're so sharp and elegant in comparison to the clothes she forced herself into. Then she gazes upward to their happy, shining faces, and feels a melancholy pang in her spirit. *God, I wish I felt like they do. I want to be glad. I want to rejoice. But I can't.* She peeks behind her and sees the kind usher who shook her hand earlier, singing and clapping to the song clanging off the walls of the building.

If only she really saw me, right now, and could sense what I'm feeling, even talk to me. Maybe then I could move past my anxiety and experience the praise and hear the preaching to come.

Loretta dutifully hangs in there. But minutes later, on the edge of losing what composure she had left, she slips out the way she came in, unnoticed because everyone else was lost in their own worship.

Whatever type of church you attend, this scenario has likely happened a lot more than once in your Sunday services. Church environments, especially those with a more charismatic flavor, are not comfortable places for those who are mentally ill. It's noisy and sometimes crowded. How attendees look and act suggest expected standards of appearance and behavior that can seem rigid and cause a person dealing with mental illness to feel awkward and even disapproved of. It could be from something as basic as clothing: people have told me, "I can't come to church because I don't have anything to wear." But it's more often caused by a sense, triggered by some sort of emotional trauma, that they just don't belong there. A friend who has dealt with situational depression told me how he, like our fictional Loretta, had to leave an Assembly of God church service, two songs into the morning worship, because he couldn't stand how happy everyone was while he was still mourning from the recent death of his mother. I, too, knew I couldn't go to church on Mother's Day Sunday just weeks after Mommy had died—and you'll recall how I forced myself to go to church after standing in my closet and sobbing for the longest time.

Of course, sadness is just one of a myriad of emotions a mentally ill person deals with in the context of their condition. Someone with depression can experience choking despair. A person dealing with PTSD can be piercingly sensitive to sounds and lights. A schizophrenic will hear things that aren't there, and a paranoid person will perceive things that aren't. A bipolar individual can quickly go from dizzying heights of happiness to sinking depths of gloom. Place any of these people into an upbeat church environment and it's easy to understand why they have a hard time or feel the need to leave.

Had Loretta been able to stay through the worship service to hear the preaching, she may have confronted another problem. Many mentally ill people can misperceive and filter the sermon through their various symptoms. This can often cause them to feel condemned or guilty, believing they need to get busy doing more work for the Lord to somehow "heal" their issues. Now that I've been diagnosed with depression and PTSD, I can look all the way back to my adolescent church experiences and see that I was likely experiencing mental illness symptoms that left me feeling out of sorts and out of place. Exhortations from others to "just have faith and pray through" weren't adequate by themselves to offset the traumas I felt stemming from Daddy's alcoholism and my parent's fighting.

As an adult dealing with the on-again, off-again drama of my marriage, I've lost count of the times I got myself to church,

Exhortations from others to "just have faith and pray through" weren't adequate by themselves to offset the traumas I felt.

just to hear a message from my pastor on standing strong during trial, and thought, *What's wrong with me that I can't persevere? I'm here because I'd feel guilty if I wasn't here, and I'm hearing that I gotta do this and gotta feel that. But I'm dying on the inside.* Sadly, there were even times when Ellison and I had met with the pastor during the week to seek counsel about our marriage, only to hear him share in the Sunday message the exact issues we'd discussed with him just days earlier (and his opinions that were decidedly pro-Ellison and made me out to be the bad guy). It was embarrassing, I felt like everyone knew our business, and it made me leery to trust my pastor or ever go to him again.

The expectations I felt as a worker in the churches I attended also left no room for dealing with my mental state. I routinely took my kids to church sick, burning up with fever, and laid them on the back pew because I felt I couldn't miss the service—and I better not dare talk to anyone about it because no one else was going to understand how I felt.

How to love our Lorettas

I'm convinced there are ways we can let the Lorettas who visit our churches know they are loved and cared for, without necessarily having to change our preferred church's service style or presentation. It all comes back to what Loretta was thinking when she looked back at the usher: *If only she really saw me ... could sense what I'm feeling ... even talk to me.* The key is being aware that there are mentally ill individuals and families dealing with mental illness in our congregations, and then developing a plan of action to watch for them and minister to their needs.

A great way to do this is to train ushers, or other members of the church who serve in hospitality or prayer, how to recognize when others are experiencing anxiety or other symptoms of mental illness—and then respond personally. What I would've given for someone in church to have known me well enough to come up to me in the pew and say, "Sister Jacki, are you okay? Is something going on? Maybe we can go together over to the Fellowship Hall right now if the service is too much for you. Do you want to do that?"

The day Mommy died, I went to my local grocery store to get some food and supplies. Being the creature of habit that I am, I chose the checkout line with a clerk I almost always picked because she had a welcoming face. Otherwise, I didn't know any-thing else about her.

"How are you doing today?" she inquired with a smile.

"To tell you the truth," I replied, "I'm not doing good at all. My mother died this morning."

This woman I did not know looked me straight in the eyes. "I'm so sorry." Genuine compassion toned her words. "Can I give you a hug?"

My heart longed for the embrace of this nearly-total stranger. "Yes, you can," I said, my voice cracking. "But I'm going to cry."

"That's okay," she said as she made her way around the counter. "Just cry."

And right there, in the middle of the crowded grocery store, we hugged and I cried. It was beautiful. Every single time I've been back to that store since then, that clerk has asked me how I'm doing, and sometimes just acknowledged, "Today is not a good day, is it?" She didn't require a deep, intimate knowledge of me or my life. But she was sensitive and compassionate. Not surprisingly, she later told me that she is a Christian—though I didn't know that or need to know it when she offered her caring embrace that sorrowful day.

This is what should happen in our churches. I shouldn't walk into the sanctuary of my church on Sunday morning feeling dis-couraged, depressed, or worse, and not have someone notice what's going on, just enough to offer a sincere, "How are you?" In those moments, I don't want to pray about it. I don't want a prog-nosis. I just want someone to say something that will make me feel better and assured that I am loved and cared for. They don't need to know all the answers. They just need to be there. When I had cancer, there were a few close friends who literally stopped calling me. Later, they told me it was because they didn't know what to say. I asked them, "What would you have said to me if I didn't have cancer? Just because I had cancer didn't change the fact that I wanted to talk to you—not about the cancer, but what you did over the weekend or how your kids are doing?" In other words, I wanted simple, normal conversation and the knowledge that they cared for me.

Granted, people like Loretta and me may try to cover up our emotions and hide our true condition. That's when I feel the Holy Spirit can and will intervene to help the person trained to reach out to the mentally ill person or family member. In my church, I have often experienced being led by the Spirit, even in the midst of my own depression or anxiety, to connect with someone else I observe in the congregation who is dealing with the same symptoms. I call it my "ministry of hugs." When embracing someone, God through His Spirit enables me to actually feel what the other person is feeling—and sometimes even take it away from them and upon myself, like the passing of a baton, to help the other individual be less burdened and feel better. I've even had people cling on to me and then express, "I really just needed a hug today." It's an incredible sensation, and while it's not always easy on me to take on someone else's sadness or worry, God always helps me to then give it to Him to carry and heal. It's a unique gifting, and one I believe others can operate in as the Lord leads and equips.

Another way to love your church's Lorettas is to make sure she understands that her mental illness does not mean she lacks faith in God, is deficient in her trust in Him, or absent of worth in the church. Heartbreakingly, misconceptions about mental illness in some African American churches has caused those with mental illness to question their very relationship with God. The stigma they feel creates a sense of shame to where they believe they have been looked down upon by the pastor, other church members, or even God Himself.

When I felt this way in the past, I continued to teach or serve in my church despite the crushing weight of despair from the guilt and rejection I carried. Because my mental illness wasn't being recognized, and therefore I wasn't being encouraged to seek professional help for my condition, I'd just pray for God to give me some sort of fresh "anointing" to take it all away. This tendency to seek purely spiritual solutions to address mental illness discourages people from seeking the professional help they need.

In the end, it is the responsibility of church pastors and leaders to be cautious not to ostracize those in their congregations who are suffering from or dealing with mental illness. Such behavior sends an unmistakable message that our perspective about others, and even the church's priorities, are out of whack.

I think of the story from the book of Matthew when Jesus was approached by two demon-possessed men:

> "They were so violent that no one could pass that way. 'What do you want with us, Son of God?' they shouted. 'Have you come here to torture us before the appointed time?' Some distance from them a large herd of pigs was feeding. The demons begged Jesus, 'If you drive us out, send us into the herd of pigs.' He said to them, 'Go!' So they came out and went into the pigs, and the whole herd rushed down the steep bank into the lake and died in the water. Those tending the pigs ran off, went into the town and reported all this, including what had happened to the demon-possessed men. Then the whole town went out to meet Jesus. And when they saw him, they pleaded with him to leave their region." (Matthew 8:28-34)

What makes this story tragic is the fact that the townspeople were more upset about losing a herd of pigs than they were concerned about the two men Jesus had delivered. Sometimes church leaders and pastors can be more worried about the well-being of the church's programs, or even about how many people are attending Sunday services, than about giving attention to the people in the congregation that need help because of mental illness. The Bible is clear that we should never turn our backs on those who have conditions or situations we may not want to deal with. To ostracize others, for any reason, can undermine opportunities for the Lord to minister to them. Notice this example, also from the book of Matthew:

It is the responsibility of church pastors and leaders to be cautious not to ostracize those in their congregations who are suffering from or dealing with mental illness.

"A Canaanite woman from that vicinity came to him, crying out, 'Lord, Son of David, have mercy on me! My daughter is demon-possessed and suffering terribly.' Jesus did not answer a word. So his disciples came to him and urged him, 'Send her away, for she keeps crying out after us.' He answered, 'I was sent only to the lost sheep of Israel.' The woman came and knelt before him. 'Lord, help me!' she said. He replied, 'It is not right to take the children's bread and toss it to the dogs.' 'Yes it is, Lord," she said. 'Even the dogs eat the crumbs that fall from their master's table.' Then Jesus said to her, 'Woman, you have great faith! Your request is granted.' And her daughter was healed at that moment." (Matthew 15:22-28)

We must realize that every human being is a unique creation of God longing to be touched by the reality of His love. Like Loretta, they want to be cared for by others in the church in a way that causes them to get help for their mental illness, while at the same time seek comfort from the One who said, "Come to me, all you who are weary and burdened, and I will give you rest. Take my yoke upon you and learn from me, for I am gentle and humble in heart, and you will find rest for your souls. For my yoke is easy and my burden is light." (Matthew 11:28-30) At the same time, the Lorettas in our midst don't want to be defined by their mental illness. I often tell others, "I have mental illness, but I'm still a whole being." PTSD is not who I am. It's what I have. If someone wants to share something happy or positive that the Lord has done for them, I never want them to hesitate to do so because I deal with depression or may even be depressed at that moment. In fact, their praise will likely encourage me.

Loving Their Loretta: Michael and Maria

I have also been encouraged to see how congregation members, and even leaders within some churches, have begun to speak up about how mental illness is either affecting them or impacting their loved ones. Not surprisingly, two of those leaders are Pastors Michael and Maria. In fact, this couple who were so accepting of me and my conditions are now dealing with their own mental health issue in the form of something common to church leaders: burnout.

In June 2017, they resigned as our pastors after 24 uninterrupted years of church ministry. I say "uninterrupted" because they had never taken extended time off, usually referred to in church circles as a "sabbatical," in all that time. When they did go on a vacation, Michael said it was nothing to "renew or revive ourselves, but to go and do so that we can get back and do church." He revealed that he was tired and was at a point where he felt he had nothing to give. "I didn't want to give the people of the church anything of me, but everything of God. On certain Sundays, I preached a message that I knew was all God. Maria told me it was a great message, and I'd be, 'Wow, Lord knows I didn't have that.'" But Michael was so exhausted that it bred frustration within him. "God always showed up on behalf of His people when I was not feeling it and having a hard time doing it. I got mad. 'Lord, what about me?' I asked. 'I'm tired. I'm broken. I feel I need a break. But look at what you're doing. The message is touching and changing lives, but it's doing nothing for me.'"

Michael said every pastor sees good, bad, and ugly days, but not every pastor is good at taking care of themselves as they should. "As pastors, Maria and I have always been more concerned for the people than for ourselves, which sounds good, but on the other hand is not. When you don't take care of yourself, sometime it's going to get to you. We were always good at taking our needs and our family time and putting them aside so we could be there for the church," he admitted. "Pastors can be easily upset at their church people and never say it. They hold grudges, unforgiveness, hurts, and bitterness that, if never dealt with, can come out and get them. Pastors also feel like they carry the weight of the whole church on their shoulders, and when it gets too heavy, burnout comes. Pastors are often asked to do more than they should do."

While Maria continued going to church services after they began their sabbatical, Michael did not. He didn't go to church for five full months. He got more involved in coaching basketball, something he had already been doing for a while, and even coached his daughter's club team at the same time she was playing for her high school. He believes he has benefitted from the perspective of "seeing the Christian life from the other side of the pulpit."

"As pastor, I got so frustrated with people where one Sunday you saw them, then the next two Sundays you didn't. They were doing family time on Sunday, and I'd think, 'What? Come to church for family time!' But now I get it. There are Sundays where you just don't want to get out of bed. When our daughter started playing basketball games on Sunday, it was such a hard pull for us. We wanted to make her games, but we had to be in church. After we stepped away, that was not an issue," Michael said. "If we were to ever pastor again, I won't allow myself to get so frustrated with the every-now-and-then church attender. I'm enjoying my rest."

The sabbatical has caused Maria to become more introspective about her spirituality. "As Christians, we go to church. We pay tithes. We worship. I was born and raised Assembly of God, and I never asked why. I just did it," she said. "Now I'm able to think, 'What do I need in my life? What do I believe?' I'm digging for truth, and as I do, it's confirming my faith." Maria added that she never had the luxury of doing that while she was pastoring but is now reaffirming core aspects of what she believes and why. She feels encouraged by the Lord. "As a pastor, you're expected to have spiritual disciplines. But as only a Christ-follower, it all goes to your personal convictions, and that's where you dig deep. We're still learning and searching," she said of her and her husband.

As of the writing of this book, Michael and Maria had no plans to return to pastoring, but they do believe there is a stigma in churches toward those who are dealing with mental illness. "I serve a real God in a real world," Michael said, "and with that statement, mental health issues are real. In the church, we have this mindset that because God is God, illnesses and sicknesses can and should be quickly healed or taken care of—and that if it doesn't happen, then there's something wrong with your faith or your life. The mentality is that Christians shouldn't go through that because we serve God." He added, "In some churches, there is a belief that if you're sick, it's sin. I don't believe that. Some look at mental illness as a curse, and I don't believe that."

What Michael does believe is that sin can be a *contributing* cause because sin exists in a world where negative things happen to good people. "A person can be killed by a drunk driver because they were in the wrong place at the wrong time. It wasn't that the person killed was living in sin, but the world of sin caught him that night." He also feels God can bring healing to people with mental illness through whatever process it takes, including therapy and medication. Speaking of me, he said, "PTSD is part of life, and unfortunately it hit her. But there's a real God in Heaven who will help her through it. Another thing we've said as pastors is, 'Everything you are and everything you go through is always for somebody else.' Her experience makes Jacki the perfect person to love on someone with mental illness."

Maria said she believes the stigma in the church shows itself when mental illness is seen as a weakness of faith. "Bible verses tell us to renew our mind and that the joy of the Lord is our strength, and when a person goes through mental illness, it can be thought that they doubt their faith. They wonder, 'Where is my strength, my foundation, now that I'm going through this?'" she said. "Jacki may have been afraid to tell us about her mental illness because she'd be showing us her weakness, that she was broken. But I told her, 'You're not broken. You may have a little bit of cracks.' I remember sharing about this old Japanese fable where if their vases were cracked, they mended them with gold. Jacki is being mended with God's gold."

Looking back at that night in the restaurant when Ellison and I told Michael and Maria about my mental illness and my therapy, I was indeed afraid. But it turns out they were, too.

"Usually as a pastor, when you get that kind of dinner request, it's negative; something is wrong with us as pastors, or someone is going to leave the church," Michael said. "Since it was Jacki and Ellison, we knew what good friends we were and the depth of our relationship. Maria and I were going in with a 'We'll see what happens' attitude, but we went in with the mindset that if they felt it was their time to go to another church, we were going to be okay with it. We knew they wanted God to control their lives and to do His will."

So when I told them about my mental illness issues and my therapy, their first reaction was one of relief. "Maria was like, 'Whew.' I thought, 'That's all? I can handle that.' I think I even said, 'We should have PTSD, too. We're crazy like you,'" Michael said, laughing. "When somebody shares something like that, number

I was their Loretta— and Michael and Maria knew how to love me.

one, they don't have to, and number two, they must love us enough to tell us. There was no way we were going to say anything against what a doctor had told her or what she was doing to get treatment. We just wanted her to know, 'We're here for you. You don't have to go through this alone. We are going to be your friends, not just your pastors."

"We told her that communication was going to be a huge thing for us," Maria added, "because we needed her to teach us while she's learning, and to tell us what she's feeling and thinking, because we're there to serve her in the healing process. We were focused on, 'What's next? Let's get on the journey for your healing.'"

I was their Loretta—and Michael and Maria knew how to love me. As pastors, they were models of how church leaders should respond to someone with mental illness. As non-pastors on their ongoing sabbatical, they are a model of how to accept and cope with their own mental challenges.

Chapter 9

According to the Library of Congress (LOC), the African American spiritual (also called the Negro Spiritual) constitutes one of the largest and most significant forms of folk songs in the United States. Sung by slaves chained together on the fields of plantations, songs such as "Swing Low, Sweet Chariot" and "Deep Down in my Heart" provided the soundtrack of the American south from the late 1700s through to the end of legalized slavery in the 1860s and beyond. One such song, "Steal Away to Jesus," indicated the longing for freedom, both in this life and the next:

Steal away, steal away, steal away to Jesus
Steal away, steal away home
I ain't got long to stay here

My Lord, He calls me
He calls me by the thunder
The trumpet sounds within-a my soul
I ain't got long to stay here

Green trees are bending
Po' sinner stand a-trembling

The trumpet sounds within-a my soul
I ain't got long to stay here
(COURTESY: WWW.NEGROSPIRITUALS.COM)

The LOC website states that "the term 'spiritual' is derived from the King James Bible translation of Ephesians 5:19: 'Speaking to yourselves in psalms and hymns and spiritual songs, singing and making melody in your heart to the Lord.' The form has its roots in the informal gatherings of African slaves in 'praise houses' and outdoor meetings called 'brush arbor meetings,' 'bush meetings,' or 'camp meetings.'"

From this tragic yet richly beautiful legacy of spiritual expression, African American people have relied heavily on religion and their church experiences to help them get through the toughest times. Today, it is often still the go-to in the African American community, a place where family, community, and spiritual belief tend to be great sources of strength and support. However, many African Americans can rely on faith, family, and social communities for emotional support—and neglect turning to health care professionals, even when medical or therapeutic treatment is clearly necessary.

This was the case for my Daddy. He died from an advanced stage of prostate cancer that might have been prevented had he simply gone to the doctor early enough. His generation referred to cancer as "The Big C," and while he was terrified of the disease, he was even more terrified of medical professionals. He grew up in the South and never graduated high school, so Daddy had trouble understanding doctors, and that lack of understanding bred fear. By the time he did go to the doctor, he received his cancer diagnosis, was treated successfully (though he never told me specifics), and went into remission—but not for long. When it returned, he called and asked me to be his medical proxy, even though he was in New York and I was in California. But by the time I got involved, though, the cancer was too far along. It had spread into his bones, and he had no more than several months left. It was too late for chemotherapy or radiation. All that was left was to ease his suffering. At the end, he didn't have to be removed from life support, but died on his own.

Daddy wasn't a spiritual man, but his behavior mirrors many African American Christians who allow fear of doctors, or just plain stubbornness, to keep them from getting the help they need. One woman I knew in church told me she had been diagnosed with diabetes but refused to "claim" it, and therefore wasn't going to get medical treatment. "You don't have to 'claim' anything," I told her. "Your pancreas is telling you that you have diabetes." But she didn't listen. Sadly, she slowly killed herself because she rejected doctor's orders, deciding instead to only "trust in God." She didn't even want to do dialysis. I said, "You just need to trust God—and hook up to that machine!"

Letting our legacy help

If anything, this tendency is worse when it comes to mental illness. We'd much rather "pray away" symptoms or "lean on the Lord" than actually see a therapist, let alone take medication. There are a couple of reasons for this. In the Bible, people were miraculously healed, and there are modern-day instances were Christians have been supernaturally delivered from diseases of all kinds. Therefore, to not believe for your own healing is seen as having a lack of faith. The church is also a safe zone and viewed as being therapeutic in and of itself. So if you're going to church, why should you seek therapy anywhere else?

Please don't misunderstand me. The Bible works. Prayer

works. Church and belief play a prominent role in fostering physical, emotional, and mental well-being. But those things don't have to be the end all. Faith and spirituality are essential, but they should not be the only option we pursue. In fact, our spiritual practices can be a strong assist to treatment. Our spiritual legacy can help us have the courage to get additional help, empower us during treatment, and inspire and equip us to maintain ongoing medical or psychological regimens when our condition has been addressed.

This is where our faith communities and spiritual leadership need to provide vital support to eliminate ignorance and isolation. In some cases, this is already being done. Many churches have started groups that deal with grief. My church in California launched a spin-off from the women's ministry support group for breast cancer that broadened the outreach to include those dealing with any form of cancer. I spoke to that group a couple of years ago. There are churches that now have groups that minister to divorced people, and even groups of nurses who offer wellness classes and exercise and diet advice to the congregation and its leaders. One organization in Tucson that conducted past community-wide health fairs even planned a first-ever mental health fair in late spring 2018. The motivation: the prevailing stress people feel regarding events such as school shootings and other traumas.

Church and belief play a prominent role in fostering physical, emotional, and mental well-being. But those things don't have to be the end all.

These are all wonderful! But just as there are people in our churches with cancer or diabetes or any other number of physical ailments, there are also people who have mental illnesses or loved ones who do. Yet how many churches host specific support groups for the mentally ill or their families? This could be done through leadership connecting with fellow Christian therapists to oversee the group or provide training to other leaders within the church on how to interact and connect with people who have or are dealing with mental illness. Certainly, those who are successfully dealing with their own mental illnesses such as PTSD or depression could also get involved.

If a church takes the positive step of referring its congregants to mental health professionals for treatment, it needs to openly support their member's use of therapy and medications, safe and moral means of dealing with their conditions as opposed to self-medicating or worse. Likewise, churches must provide ongoing support for its members who are dealing with mental illness and not just hand them off to the system, private or government. Abandoning them to the system sends a clear message that the church has nothing to offer people in times of real crisis.

As I was reflecting on this need within our Christian churches, I was reminded of the message the Lord gave the prophet Jeremiah:

> "This is the word that came to Jeremiah from the Lord: 'Go down to the potter's house, and there I will give you my message.' So I went down to the potter's house, and I saw him working at the wheel. But the pot he was shaping from the clay was marred in his hands; so the potter formed it into another pot, shaping it as seemed best to him. Then the word of the Lord came to me. He said, 'Can I not do with you, Israel, as this potter does?' declares the Lord. 'Like clay in the hand of the potter, so are you in my hand, Israel.'" (Jeremiah 18:1-6)

From this passage of Scripture, we see that the potter (our Lord) knows the clay with which He is working. We can be "marred" by anything—including mental illness—but He doesn't throw us away as though we are useless. He continues to use us and shape us into what He needs to complete our purpose and destiny!

Now look at this passage from the book of Isaiah:

"The Spirit of the Sovereign Lord is on me, because the Lord has anointed me to proclaim good news to the poor. He has sent me to bind up the brokenhearted, to proclaim freedom for the captives and release from darkness for the prisoners, to proclaim the year of the Lord's favor and the day of vengeance of our God, to comfort all who mourn, and provide for those who grieve in Zion—to bestow on them a crown of beauty instead of ashes, the oil of joy instead of mourning, and a garment of praise instead of a spirit of despair. They will be called oaks of righteousness, a planting of the Lord for the display of his splendor." (Isaiah 61:1-3)

This Scripture should be a mantra for all Christians, but in African American churches it is usually seen as applying only to someone who is stepping into a ministry position or calling within the church. That's not true. The prophet Isaiah here gives us directives that all believers in God should follow. Christians are supposed to be the very ones who are the most compassionate, helpful, and giving. Yet when we turn our backs on others and tell them to "just pray about it," we fail to live out His Great Commission (Matthew 28:16-20) and share the redemptive grace of Jesus. Even more, this passage is a call to *all of us* to help those in need—and that includes those who have mental illness or their families. This is vital because people who are mentally ill or dealing with mental illness are just waiting to be recognized, affirmed, and given worth within our churches.

I'll never forget the moment this was hammered home to me. I was speaking once again at an annual women's conference in San Jose, California. It was a regular and treasured event on my schedule, hosted by a longtime friend. I was out in the lobby with other conference vendors when I overheard my friend talking to an attendee, a young woman in her twenties.

People who are mentally ill or dealing with mental illness are just waiting to be recognized, affirmed, and given worth within our churches.

Apparently, there had been a mishap where her scheduled roommate didn't need the lodging, leaving her without a place to stay.

I walked over and asked my friend, "Have you assigned anyone to stay with me in my room?"

"No," she responded. "As one of our speakers, you have a room to yourself."

I looked at the woman and smiled. "Well, then she can stay with me."

My friend asked if I was sure, and I said that I was. Then I introduced myself to the woman. "You don't do anything crazy in your sleep, do you?" I kidded.

That seemed to set her at ease. She laughed. "No, ma'am."

I responded, "Well, I talk in my sleep, but I promise I won't bother you."

We joined a group of people to grab a bite to eat and got to know one another. I learned that she had two boys ages two and seven and that she was separated from her husband. She asked what course I was going to be teaching, and I told her it was the marriage class. When we got to our room, she again thanked me for my hospitality, then added, "I'm really glad I didn't have to go back home this weekend. I'm currently living in a women's shelter for domestic violence."

I still had some preparation to do for my class and had my computer open, but I sensed she had more to share. "I'll just do some reading," she said, noticing I had work to do. "I try to read the Bible to settle down every night because I have a hard time sleeping."

"I'd imagine so," I replied, "living in a shelter."

"Yeah," she said. "Sometimes I feel like I'm in this fog or black hole."

My spirit quickened. *Okay, God,* I thought with a thrill. *You set this up for us, didn't you?*

I turned toward her and encouraged her share more, after which she declared, "I think I have postpartum—no, that's not it. It's something else that begins with a P"

"PTSD?" I asked.

"Yeah, that's it!" Hope tinged her voice.

I grinned. "Well, I'm in the process of writing another book, and it's about that exact thing." I told her a synopsis of *Cancer With Grace*, then said, "In it, you meet a woman who is full of faith. In my second book, you wouldn't even recognize that lady."

Then I told her all about my bouts with depression, PTSD, and about my therapy. It was the first time I'd shared any of those details with a stranger—and we stayed up talking until two in the morning. It was a God moment where I realized that I was going to need to start talking about these issues openly. Even more, it was a moment where I saw the recognition, affirmation, and value that sharing my experiences brought to my unplanned roommate.

Before we finally went to sleep, she asked, "Can I call you Mom?"

"Sure," I said.

And I knew. The Diva was going to reveal—and it was going to be glorious.

At the end of one of our sessions as we neared the completion of this manuscript, my editor said to me, "You're a key player in the existing movement of God." I freaked out! *What? Me? Key in God's movement?* I thought of the biblical giants that truly were vital in the movement of God – Moses, David, Deborah, Paul, just to name a few—and as I tried to wrap my head around all of that, God showed me some incredible insights.

In Moses, we find someone whose personality was shaped by God. The Lord didn't change who Moses was; He didn't give him new abilities and strengths. He took Moses as he was and molded him to suit His purposes. Moses was the greatest Jewish leader who set the exodus into motion.

David is remembered and respected for his heart for the Lord. More than anything, David had an unchangeable belief in the faithful and forgiving nature of God, which made him quick to confess his sins. His life is the example that we should be willing to honestly admit our mistakes.

Deborah had a remarkable relationship with God. She didn't deny or resist her position in the culture as a woman and wife, but she never allowed herself to be hindered by it, either. Her story shows that God can accomplish great things through people who are willing to be led by Him.

In Paul we find no other person, apart from Jesus Himself, who shaped the history of Christianity more than he did. Paul's personal encounter with Jesus changed his life. But he never lost his fierce intensity. Instead, he channeled it for the gospel. The lives Paul touched were changed and challenged by meeting Christ through him.

How in the world do I, Jacquelyn D. Murray, live up to these giants in biblical history? How can God use me? Again, I heard

that concise, unmistakable, quiet voice say, "That's what I do, Jacki—use people."

How can God use me? Again, I heard that concise, unmistakable, quiet voice say, "That's what I do, Jacki—use people."

Moses is an example that God prepares, then uses. His timetable is life-sized. He does His greatest work through frail people. We share and identify in David's failures. We can also have his confidence that God can use us, too. Deborah reminds us to be available to both God and others. We learn from her to spend our efforts on what we *can* do rather than worry about

what we can't. She challenges us to be wise leaders. Paul was transformed by God from the prime persecutor of Christians to the foremost preacher for Christ. He was sensitive to God's leading, and despite his strong personality, always did as God directed.

So *yes*, I am a key player in the next movement of God. I make no apologies for my depression, anxiety, or PTSD. I'm broken. But I will not be ashamed for something that I can't help or change. I can no more change the imbalances in my brain than my eye color. I am who I am—and still, with all my frailties, inabilities, flaws, and illnesses, He *can* use me! And He can use you, too!

Here's how, as I now reveal the ministry, *His* ministry, that He's chosen me to share through five specific speaking presentations.

You're amazing to others, but not yourself

I have discovered that those of us dealing with mental illness are pretty amazing people—to others, if not to ourselves. We're often the "go to" person for others but have no one to "go to" ourselves. We tell others not to worry about what other people think, but secretly we worry about what others think about us if they knew we were mentally ill. We give great advice to everyone else, but not necessarily to ourselves. We say "yes" to others and "no" to ourselves. Finally, we have bought into the hype that we must work past our hurts and feelings in order to feel successful and that we have a purpose. In "Why Amazing People Can Be Depressed," I will speak to each one of these tendencies and share what the Bible says about each one so that you can be more effective at self-care while still caring for others.

You're sick, not crazy

This is one of the first misconceptions many people dealing with mental illness must overcome. The fact is, mental illness is just that—an illness. We're not crazy, we're sick, and just like those with physical sickness, we don't want the illness. Think about it: if you had a fellow church member who was diagnosed with diabetes, you'd encourage them to take the necessary health and dietary precautions to manage their condition, right? The same exhortation applies to those dealing with mental health issues. In "People Who Have Mental Illness Are Not Crazy...They're Sick," I will talk about Scripture has to say about encouraging one another in love, as well as provide tips on how to develop and maintain a positive outlook as you cope with mental illness in your life or family.

You need help, not guilt

James 2:14-17 provides a poignant illustration of what happens when we only apply faith to a situation without any tangible, practical deeds to go with it. I'm convinced that Christians must stop sending those dealing with mental illness into hopeless despair by guilting them into not seeking the help they need. If we believe God is the creator of everything and everyone, then He also created therapy, therapists, and the medicine that help treat mental illness. In "Seeking Help Does Not Demonstrate a Lack of Faith," I will address how foolish it is to question how God chooses to heal, restore, and deliver—then teach how our prayers should be for God to direct those dealing with mental illness to the right people and situations that will bring them to wholeness, wellness, and healing of mind, body, and spirit.

You need to be heard and loved

It's entirely normal to experience a flurry of emotions when you or a loved one is diagnosed with a mental illness. Guilt, shame, disbelief, fear, anger, and grief are all common, and acceptance can take time. Family members can be an especially invaluable resource for individuals coping with mental illness, but only as they educate themselves about mental illness to inform their actions. In "No One Is Immune from Dealing with Mental Illness," I will speak to the stigmas surrounding mental illness and how to overcome them through open, honest communication and setting realistic expectations. Individuals with mental illnesses still have an identity and a voice desperate to be heard by those closest to them. The more we learn, the easier it is to provide the kind of loving assistance that benefits everyone involved.

You need to get help early

Contrary to some erroneous assumptions, not everyone dealing with mental illness is prone to a nervous breakdown, homicidal, or even suicidal. However, if they don't seek treatment, something tragic could happen. When treated early and effectively, those with mental illness often lead productive, successful lives with minor disruption. Yet because of the shame, stigma, and guilt associated with mental illness, many do not seek treatment as quickly as they could have or should have. In "Mental Illness and Suicide, Homicide, and Nervous Breakdown," I will share about my suicide attempt, why I was driven to it, and how I overcame it. Then I will talk about the importance of the Christian church replacing assumptions with facts, and stigmas with acceptance and communication.

Finally, I will make myself available via my website for "Encounters with The Diva," where I will interact personally with those who need a ready ear to hear about their struggles with mental illness and a sympathetic heart with whom to share their experiences. I'm not a therapist or even an expert on mental health, but I have been through it and would love to talk with you. I invite you to join me at www.jacquelyndmurray.com

About the
Author

Jacquelyn D. Murray is a writer, speaker, and teacher. She works in ministries to women at Gideon Full Gospel Baptist Church in Tucson, Arizona under the leadership of Bishop LaTresa Jester, and also serves as a member of the ministerial team and the praise and worship team. Jacki is also a florist, enjoys reading, traveling, spending time with family and friends and scrapbooking and other crafts. Jacki and her husband have been married for nearly 40 years and have two adult daughters. Born in White Plains, New York, Jacki is the oldest of five children.

Prayer
Journal

P lease use these pages to journal your prayers to the Lord. Ask Him to show you how you can minister to mentally ill individuals or families in your church and neighborhood. Write down His direction, begin praying specifically about what He tells you, and keep track of your conversation with God here.

In addition, if you are dealing with mental illness yourself or in your family, begin praying specifically about that condition or person. Write down His direction and your prayerful responses.

God bless you as you seek Him!

Made in the USA
Columbia, SC
22 April 2021

36620141R00089